# The Modern Theory

## of Employment, Interest and Money

**Moslem Ansarinasab**

Vali-e-Asr University of Rafsanjan

**Title:** The Modern Theory of Employment, Interest and Money

**Author:** Moslem Ansarinasab

**Cover Design:** Ali Khiabanian

**ISBN-13:** 978-1947464056

**ISBN-10:** 1947464051

**LCCN**: 2017959369

**Publisher:** American Academic Research,Glendale, CA, USA

## Brief Contents

Chapter 1: How the Economy Works?

Chapter 2: How does money work in the economy?

Chapter 3: How economic growth and business cycles come into existence?

Chapter 4: What should be done?

**Preface**

The history of human civilization is the history of human effort to find a way to make their life better. The history is full of solutions that have been found by thinkers and scientists in their attempts to facilitate the problems of human life. Economics has not been an exception to this rule, and thinkers in this field have been trying to find solutions to maximize human prosperity and welfare. Despite all these advances, economic ups and downs, inequalities in the level and quality of life, and poverty in the wealth accumulated in the planet suggests that these efforts, although worthwhile, have not yet succeeded in helping human being to reach their ultimate goals.

The history of economics is full of ideas, solutions, and creativities that have advanced the civilization of mankind. Of these, one invention is the most influential one: money. However, the invention of money by facilitating transactions paved the way for the advancement of human civilization. Accordingly, this book seeks to show how money has turned into a Frankenstein in a way that this man-made and weird creature instead of being controlled by human has dominated the human life. In fact, human is a chained captive in the face of this creature, and the captivity chains of money are slowly going to obstruct the way of breathing for mankind.

The book seeks to show how money has been a barrier to human development through its changing nature and functions, and has incited inequality and poverty, and how money has prevented economic growth and created economic ups and downs. After recognizing the problem, at the end of the book, by presenting an innovative solution, we will show how to control this rebellious creature and release humanity from the bondage of captivity and direct the free human beings to an ideal society.

We have named this book "The Modern Theory of Employment, Interest, and Money", not to say that it is a book in contrast to "The General Theory of Employment, Interest, and Money," but only because to commemorate the great thinker John Maynard Keynes, who come up with a good recognition of the problem, but his solution was not effective enough to resolve it.

**Moslem Ansarinasab**

Vali-e-Asr University of Rafsanjan,
E-mail: m.ansarinasab@vru.ac.ir

# Chapter 1
# How the Economy Works?

How the economy works? This the most basic question in the field of economy. Answering this question sheds light on the many questions and guides us through finding solutions to economic challenges. It also brings up some other questions about the essential dynamics underlying economy and how these dynamics operate. For this, we should start from transactions as the smallest and the most fundamental constituent of economy. How each transaction is valuated has been eluding the economists for many years.

The value of the commodities in the commodity market is the price of the commodities while the value of the production agent in the labor market is the wages paid to the laborers. This raises these questions: what is the fair price for commodities? How much is the fair wages for the labor force is the labor market? On what basis are they set? Several theories have been proposed by economists in this case, the most popular of which defines the value of the provided commodity or labor in form of the necessary labor for production of that commodity or service. In other words, this theory states that 'value is the labor spent for production'. It suggests that if in comparison with B commodity, twice as much as labor is needed for production of A commodity, the price of A would be double that of B. Similarly, if A works twice as much as B, they must accordingly receive twice as much wages.

We here attempt to have a critical view of this theory to complete it. Any theory that relates the price of each commodity to the labor spent for its production or the wages of each individual to their working hours fails to consider the quality of the performance rendered by any individual. Quality-wise, different individuals show different degrees of performance quality which makes it essentially impossible to compare two different undertakings. As a matter of fact, there is no single criterion for comparing the outputs of different undertakings and different individuals with different degrees of specialty.

The theory that associates the price with the labor spent for commodity production and in the same vein the wages as the labor exercised by the labor force just manages to see half the picture. What must the labor be measured against if the value is measured by the labor? How the value of the labor is set? Let us give an example to clarify the point. Imagine that two tailors have made a shirt in one hour using the same materials. The shirt made by the first tailor has poor quality of making with an appalling design while the second tailor has managed to produce a beautiful shirt of high-quality making. Now, the prices must be the same because of equal labor spent? Moreover, must both tailors be paid the same wages because they have had the same materials and time?

In another example, let's assume two actors of different calibers and performance quality receive roles in the same movie. The first actor has produced an ordinary performance while the second one has starred in their role. Should both be paid the same wages? It goes without saying that the theory that attempts to relate the price and wages to the labor and sees the value solely in the labor just narrates half the story and ignores the other half which is dedicated to calculating the value of the labor itself.

In the first example, both tailors used the same materials in the same time. In the second example, the undertaking or the movie is the same for both actors. So what decides the wages of the individuals? There is no doubt that the wages must be different for these individuals based on their levels of expertise.

Individuals in these examples do the something which may make it easier to answer the questions on the wages. However, let's make the third example with two different commodities. Imagine that A is a mason working demanding hours on a daily basis while B has written software just in one day thanks to their innovation and creativity. How must everyone be paid? How their wages must be essentially set and how their marginal products must be valued? Differences in undertakings and expertise have made decision-making a little difficult here.

Does the theory that 'value is the labor spent for production' answer our questions? Is this theory vigorous enough to set the wages and fix the final price for the outputs of these individuals? Let us take the story a little further. B sells hundreds copies of their software each day. Even their daily income is more than A's monthly income.

Can we still insist that 'value is the labor spent for production? ' and 'does the labor alone set the price and wages?'. Now that we have learned the wages of both individuals, can we say that their wages are consistent with the criteria of fairness considering the extent and nature of their jobs? What is the fair wage-setting proportion for these two? A must be paid double as much as B if only the labor spent is the decisive criterion. B essentiality has worked for only one day but is paid on a daily basis for the sales of their software. Is that fair?

I hope so far you have been convinced that a labor-based wage fixing configuration is not compelling enough to plausibly justify how wages and prices are set in reality. How prices and wages are determined then? We have to get back to the starting point of the discussion: yes, value is the labor put in the production. This is the labor that decides the wages and prices. However, there must be some criterion for measuring the labor to allow for comparing how two individuals perform. As a matter of fact, what are the criteria for comparing the performances of different individuals? What is the criterion for measuring the labor exercised for production purposes?

As the kilogram is the criterion for measuring the mass of objects and the meter is used for measuring distances, a measurement criterion could be developed to compare the performances and the labor of different individuals to fix the price of final outputs and the wages of the labor force, a criterion that not only measures the performances of different individuals on the same task, but also could compare different tasks given to different individuals. How the value of the labor exercised by two tailors in the first example, the actors in the second example and more importantly, the value of the labor of A and

B in the third example are determined and how is their products are valuated?

These questions have clear answers. We just have to turn our looks away from the production of commodities (supply) and focus on the consumption of commodities (demand). In fact, this is the consumer who through their mental utility valuates the price of the commodities and accordingly the wages of the labor force. In the first example, although both tailors have produced the same shirt, this is the consumer that valuates their outputs. The consumer may reluctantly just pay the first 10$ while be willing to pay 50$ for the output of the second one.

To put it other way, at the time of purchase, the consumer compares the expected purchase and consumption utility of a commodity to the expected utility of a hundred other items and then valuates the given commodity in relation to them. In the second example, the producer calculates the contribution of each actor to the box office of the movie and set the wages accordingly. In other words, they answer this question: how much utility is created for the viewers by each actor. The following general rule could be expressed:

**"Price and wages are determined by the labor while the labor is valuated through expected utility"**

Now we will take a look at the third example via applying this rule. Although A was performing the strenuous task of masonry, he was being paid much less compared to B who had written some software during one single day. Is this consistent with the fairness principle? It is not fair if the labor exercised is the criterion. However, it seems that another criterion must be put in place. The measurement criteria for different individuals could be expressed as follows:

**"The value of an individual's labor is equal to the utility they create"**

A does a challenging job but the utility they create is lower than the output of B's efforts. A's labor creates utility for just one individual (or a family) but B's product are purchased by hundreds of individuals on a daily basis and acquire utility from it. Therefore, A's wages must be in proportion to the value their output has created. On the other hand, A can demand value to the extent of the payments they receive. This applies to B as well; the fair wages paid to B must be proportionate to the value their labor has produced. Moreover, B can demand value in relation to the wages they are paid.

In the above-mentioned example and in comparison to A, B has created comparatively more value for the society and thus must be paid more. They accordingly must be entitled to demanding more value. The general rule could be written as follows:

**"Every individual may demand value in proportion to the value they create for others"**

Now clearer answers could be provided for previous questions. In the first example, the tailor that created more value must have been paid more and thus is entitled to demanding more value.

In the second example, two actors have taken part in a movie but the second one has engendered more satisfaction in the viewers and thus must be paid more. They as a result are entitled to extract more value from economical commodities. Therefore it is fair that everyone is entitled to the value equal to what they have created.

Based on this principle, to determine the wages of the labor force of a factory, the wages must be in proportion to their contributions to the value created by the products of the factory for the consumers. Otherwise, if the labor force is paid less, the owner gains their share and thus enjoys more value from the economic commodities than the utility and value they have created. This is the root of all forms of inequality.

Thus if consider the whole period of life of an individual in a justice-based society, the total utility and the value they enjoy from economic commodities over their life is equal to the sum of utilities and values they have created through producing those commodities. Having said that, we on equilibrium come to the following equation:

The total value an individual has created= the total value they have enjoyed

This rule applies not only to one year, but essentially for the whole human history!

If an individual acauires more rights from the economic commodities that they have created, there is no doubt that another individual has been shortchanged in this regard. Essentially on average, an individual's expenses during one year are equal to their income during that given year. We thus have:

Value demanded= an individual's expenses

Value supplied= an individual's income

Therefore on equilibrium, an individual could demand value from economical commodities to the extent they have provided. Let us imagine that a cake baker called S bakes 5 cakes a day and sells them all to T. Therefore, S has provided value equal to 5 cakes and now is entitled to purchase commodities or more specifically demand value equal to the income obtained from 5 cakes.

If we assume that S uses the income of selling 5 cakes to have a meal in R's restaurant, we have a simple circle in which S has obtains some value and equally provides value. In other words, S converts some value to a different type of value. This is done through an individual's labor. S could be compared to a machine that receives some value and turns it into some other value of a different nature. This is true not only for one year, but also for the whole life of an individual. In other words, an individual receives a given amount of value during their life and creates a different type of value. This is also true for the individual preceding S who is R. The latter has provided S with a meal (offering value) and demands value from Q in proportion to the income.

Also, T enjoys the value they have received from purchasing 5 cakes and then provides equal value for U. This process could be re-stated on a wider scale: Q creates value for R. R enjoys the value of Q's commodity and in turn provides S with new value (a meal) through their own labor and converting the received value. S receives the value from R and converts it into new value (5 cakes) through their own labor. S gives T the new value who in turn converts it to another type of value for U.

In fact, the value created in the first place by Q goes through R, S and T through different types of labor exercised, changes in nature during this process and finally reaches U. This is just a fraction of what happens in economy every day. In other words, thousands of values are started from as many as people and constantly change in nature through different individuals. This is true for all values and all members of a society.

If we then take one year, a value that is in the hands of one individual is exchanged during the course of the year and is transformed into a new value through labor. This could be written as follows:

Total value individuals receive= Total value individuals create

$$\sum u_i = \sum w_i$$

On the other hand, total value creates by the individuals is equal:

Total values individuals create = Number of the individuals × average of the values created by any individual× the average price of each value

$$\sum u_i = N.y.P$$

We thus have:

Number of the values created: $Y = N.y$

We thus come to this:

$$\sum u_i = Y.P$$

We also come to this point:

Total values individuals receive = The frequency of exchanges of values× prices of all values at the start of the year

$$\sum w_i = M.V$$

In the end we come to this conclusion:

$$\sum w_i = \sum u_i$$

$$M.V = P.Y$$

The rules governing the transfer of values in economics could be generally stated as follows:

1. If values are not subject to new forces, they will take their courses of movement with a consistent speed.
2. Sums of the values in each period are equal to the mass of values at the start of the period multiplied by the speed mean of the value at the beginning of that period.

3. On equilibrium, there is an equal demand for values per each offer of value and vice versa.

We will study these rules in more details in the next chapter.

We so far have come to understand that the value of an individual's labor is in proportion to the utility they have created and the value one can receive equals the sums of value they have produced.

In a barter economy, the value is demanded and supplied at the same time. According to the figure 1, value provided for B by A takes place at the same time A demands value from B and thus the value demand and supply are always equal.

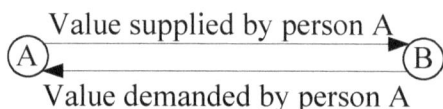

Value supplied by person A

(A) ——————————————→ (B)

Value demanded by person A

Figure 1-1: Demand and supply of values in a barter economy

Barter transactions encounter many constraints and thus human invented money to resolve the problem. The previous transaction takes the following form in presence of money.

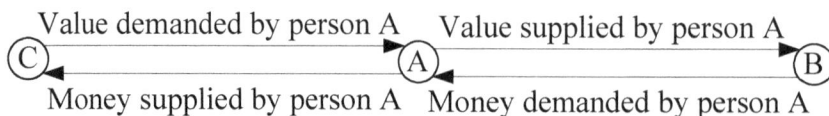

Value demanded by person A    Value supplied by person A

(C) ——————————————→ (A) ——————————————→ (B)

Money supplied by person A    Money demanded by person A

Figure 1-2: Demand and supply of values in a monetary economics

A is paid for the value they have provided B with and then demands value from C via paying them. In fact, money mediates the transactions and is like a channel through which values flow. Money is just tasked with initiating the flows of values in economics.

Despite the services money offers to economics, there are two important points:

The first point: in a barter economy no individual can demand more or less value than what they have created because demands and supplies of values happen at the same time and thus are equal. However, in a monetary economic, although no one can make requests for more value than they have provided, individuals can demand less values than their contributions if money is available. In fact, the individual can keep the demand for value in form of demand for money. Here the flows of values are stopped. Demands for money are in fact an impediment to the transfers of value in economics.

The second point: Money must be the only channel through which the flows of values are initiated in the economics. However, the problem appears when the money finds utility itself. Here, money departs from its inherent function and takes the form of an object. Money was originally invented to initiate flows of other commodities and was assigned a different function than other commodities. However, it gradually has found utility and as a result keeping the money gives individuals a sense peace. This diverts the money from its primary role as a channel to start flows of values in economics.

We will cover this issue in more details in following chapters.

# Chapter 2

# How does money work in the economy?

Economists have long been trying to find ways for explaining why economic actors make certain decisions. On what basis an individual prefers A commodity over B? Why they buy 10 units of a certain commodity but only one unit of another? On what basis an individual fixes its level of consumption and how they make decisions how much they should save or invest? These and other questions have been challenging economists during the course of history, each struggling to answer these questions and attempt to explain the factors influencing such decisions.

The introduction of the concept of 'utility' during the last two centuries has greatly contributed to the development of theories on this issue. Despite all the criticisms leveled against this concept, it has been a great help to explaining the behaviors of economic agents. Although there is no formal, exact definition for this concept, it could be generally defined as the satisfaction or the suffering resulting from decisions made by a given economic agent.

Total utility is the sums of utilities collected from the consumption of all the commodities. However, human being is inherently draws more utility from the first unit of A unit than its second unit while the second unit has more utility than the third unit. This is called the law of diminishing marginal utility in economy. The figure below shows this relation:

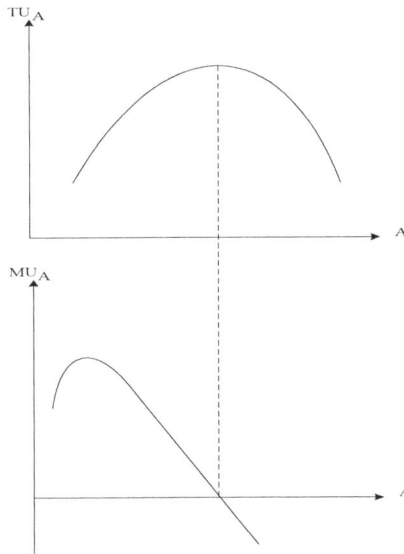

Figure 2-1: Total utility and marginal utility of commodities

Increased consumption of A commodity improves the total utility of an individual. However, this increase takes place at a slower rate. In fact, the marginal utility goes on a diminished trend and gradually drops to zero as a result of subsequent consumptions while the utility reaches its peak. This is the saturation point past which an individual receives negative utility (disutility) and their total utility drops as well. In other words, if an individual is not constrained in any way, they will use A commodity up to the saturation point.

The above-mentioned example shows the decision made by an economic agent when budget constraints are not present. However, an individual seeks to maximize the total utility which could be obtained from consuming a set of commodities when budgetary constraints are in place. For example, let us imagine that an individual plans to allocate I to purchasing A and B commodities with a view to secure maximum total utility. This individual faces this problem:

$$\text{MAX } U = \sum u(X_A, X_B)$$

$I = P_A . X_A + P_A . X_B$

Solving this question provides the equilibrium point in a way that the relative marginal utility for all the commodities will be equal for the given individual:

$$\frac{MU_A}{P_A} = \frac{MU_B}{P_B}$$

In fact, at the optimal point, the utility acquired for the last monetary unit expended on all the commodities will be equal for the given individual. This law could be generalized to all commodities, services and even decisions made on the part of decision-makers. This relation of utility covers the utility acquired from the last monetary unit expended on a loaf of bread, services obtained from owning a car, utility of acquiring new knowledge over a certain period of time, watching a movie in a movie theater, having meals in restaurants, the utility of going on a trip or using new outfits or being profited from possession of bonds, the utility of using the services of a barber shop and in general from any commodity or service.

However, there is a fine point latent in the above-mentioned arguments: the marginal utility is measured for the last monetary units and various services. Money is in fact just a criterion for measuring and transacting the values of commodities and is an exception to this law in a way. In other words, money just plays an intermediary role for transactions in most economic theories. Money-induced utility has been largely ignored in the literature on economy once the task of value measurements was assigned to a different entity. Although post-Keynesian theories have stated other tasks for money, this issue has still been ignored. As stated before, money must just be a channel for initiating flows of utility and value. However, money itself found utility over time. This is the essential question: doesn't the money increase the utility of individuals in itself?

To clarify this point, let us make an example. As said before, an individual gains more utility from two units of A commodity than one unit of such commodity and improves their total utility. But this is just half the story. In other words, imagine that an individual has 1000 monetary units while the price of each units of A commodity is 200 monetary units. Now let's take another look at the story. In the first state, the individual has one unit of A commodity and 800 monetary unit while in the second state they have two unit of A commodity and 600 monetary units. Should we accept that money has utility in itself, it is unclear if the second state necessarily increases the total utility. We will address this ambiguity later.

Let's take this the argument a little further. We learned about 'money utility' in the above-mentioned argument. Maybe this is the essential question "why should the money possess utility for its owner?". The answer is very tangible. Just put your hands in your pockets and you will find the answer. Why do you keep money? Yes, you know economics as I do: for transaction motives, precautionary motives and speculative motives. This is based on the views of John Maynard Keynes, the prominent economist. However, it seems that this analysis needs to be perfected because people never divide their demand for money in three parts and even don't know the reasons for their demands in some cases. Do you know how much you have for your transactions, how much have you put aside for the rainy day and how much for making profits? In fact it seems that dividing the demands for the remaining money of the individuals into three parts of transactions, precautionary and speculative is open to debate and often misguiding. Individuals just think about their comfort in keeping or dispensing with their money and have no divisions for the equilibrium of their money except for the utility arising from keeping the money.

Individuals essentially keep the money since life is completely open to change. They keep the money since they will be hungry and need food. They may get sick and need to pay for the treatment. An opportunity for making profits may come up etc. They need money for these reasons. By its nature, money gives comfort to an individual and thus generates utility. I therefore pool all the reasons for keeping the money in one motive which I call "comfort motive". You may disagree but this does not affect the generality of the argument.

We give a simple example to clarify the point. We have seen on several occasions that bank deposits receive for example a 2-percent interest. However, some individuals still keep some money. This seems irrational if we just consider the interest rate but is plausible if the money-induced utility comes into play. In fact, the missed interest rate for these people is insignificant compared to the utility obtained from keeping money since the joy of keeping money (with its particular characteristics) provides comfort that surpasses the profits of the missed interest rate. Individuals keep their money since it gives them comfort for any reason.

Now that we are familiar with the idea of "money utility", let's take a look at the total utility and the marginal utility of money. Does the total utility of the money increase if more money becomes available? The answer is positive. This is because money enhances the individual's utility through satisfying their "comfort motives". But the question is: when the utility of possessing money reaches its maximum or when the money marginal utility goes zero? Is money marginal utility essentially diminishing? Answering these questions completely relies on human's hierarchy of needs. Human's basic needs are more vital and have considerably more utility than other lower-tier needs. This question could also be relevant considering the diminishing marginal utility of commodities. Generally, the first monetary units have extreme marginal utility which decreases as these units increase in number. But when does the money marginal utility drop to zero? Since on one hand money is different than other commodities and is in fact a mediator for obtaining other commodities and on the other hand human's needs are known to have no limits, money marginal utility will never drop to zero or in better terms, will tend to zero in indefinitely.

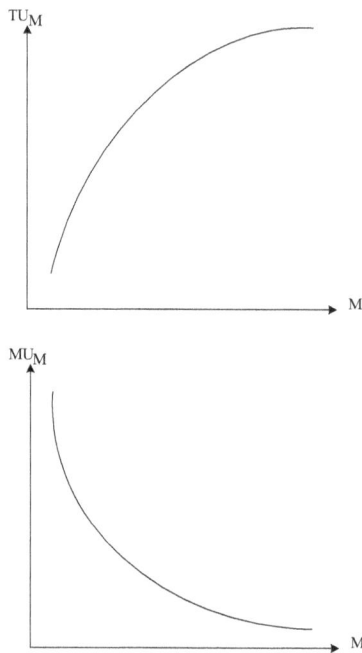

Figure 2.2: Total utility and marginal utility of money

It is then obvious that when the mass of money increases, the total utility of money ($TU_M$) still enhances since the money marginal utility ($MU_M$) is still positive. The Utility function keeps a positive slope which will be zero if only it tends to zero. These relationships are demonstrated as below:

$$MU_M = \frac{\Delta TU}{\Delta M}$$

$$MU_M \geq 0 \rightarrow TU \uparrow$$

$$\lim_{M \to \infty} MU_M = 0$$

These cases clearly distinguish the utility of money from the utility of other alternatives. Now that we have set out the differences, let's take a look at the transaction of these two in form of an indifference curve. The money mass is indicated by M while the alternatives are represented by X.

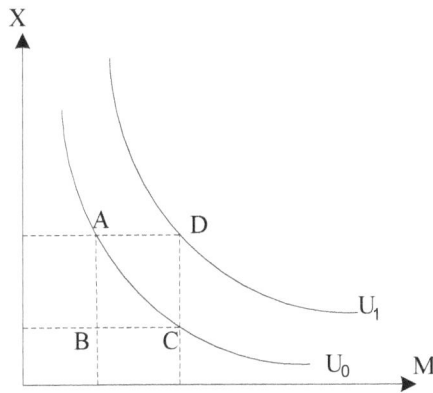

Figure 2.3: Functions of Consistent Utility

According to this figure, an individual who has lost part of their commodities (moving to B from A) will keep their utility provided that the money kept increases to a certain point (moving to C from B) and in the reverse direction. Moreover, an individual loses some of their utility as a result of cuts the in money kept. The utility will be restored to the previous level if only the utility of the replacement commodities equals to the utility losses. In other words, these two will be on the same indifference curves.

However, if the money kept stays unchanged while other commodities increase or if other commodities stay the same while the money kept increases, the individual will go up on the iso-utility curve and new baskets (D) will produce more utility for them compared to the previous baskets (A,C).

Now that the concept of slope has been defined in the previous graph, it is possible to figure out the marginal rate of money substitution and other commodities. In fact, the slope of iso-utility curve represents the marginal rate of money substitution and other commodities in each point, a rate although variable in different points, always on a descending slope.

$$MRS_{X,M} = \frac{\Delta X}{\Delta M} = -\frac{MU_M}{MU_X}$$

The individual on the other hand has to deal with certain budgetary limits or given expense functions. These limitations are set out in the following figure and formula:

$$I = r.M + p.X$$

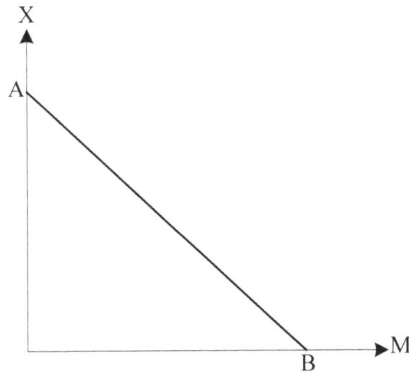

Figure 2-4: Budget Line Limits

In the point A, the individual spends all their budgets on substitute commodities (X) and purchases X=I/P amount of commodities, keeping no money in the process. In contrast, in the B point, the individual does not purchase any substitute commodity and spends all their money on keeping their money. It should be noted that the money kept by the individual (M) is more than their budget (I). In other words, if the money price is the interest rate (r), the individual can only keep M money with their whole budget (I=M.r) (for example, with a budget of one thousand units and 10% interest rate, the individual could keep ten thousand money units at maximum).

Since this explanation may seem a little complex, we provide another interpretation of the issue. In fact, the individual could purchase X amount of substitute commodity at P price and spend XP money for this. They also could Keep M amount of money and accepts M.r for this missed opportunities at the interest rate of r. The total costs could be calculated as follows:

Costs of the substitute goods+ costs of the missed opportunity=total costs

$$I = r.M + p.X$$

Either interpretation we accept, we will face the same limit or constraint which makes the individual choose between the money and its substitute commodities. In addition, the budget line slope is computed as below:

$$\text{the budget line slope} = \frac{\Delta X}{\Delta M} = -\frac{r}{p}$$

Now we return to maximizing the individual's utility. The individual struggles to produce the highest iso-utility curve while keeping the budget constraints into the account. According to this figure, the best decision is made at the point E where the individual picks $X_E, M_E$ basket.

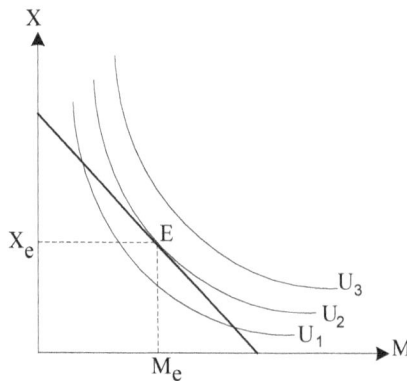

Figure 2-5: The tangent point of the budget line and the iso-utility curve

The utility of the individual will be at the maximum level. This point is unique since the slope of the iso-utility curve equals that of the budget line and thus this condition must be fulfilled before reaching the utility point.

$$\frac{MU_M}{MU_X} = \frac{r}{p} \rightarrow \frac{MU_M}{r} = \frac{MU_X}{p}$$

In other words, on iso-utility, the relative money marginal utility equals the relative marginal utility of substitute commodities which maximizes the total utility of the individual (sums of the utilities obtained from both the money and its substitute commodities).

Now that we have become familiar with maximizing the individual's utility and their optimal basket, it is time to address the effects of lowering the interest rate on the individual's optimal basket. Lowering the interest rates will move the budget constraints to the right of the graph, tangent to higher utility curves. It is obvious that the individual can still purchase X=I/P substitute commodities but they could keep more money (M=I/r) because the interest rate (r) is lower than before.

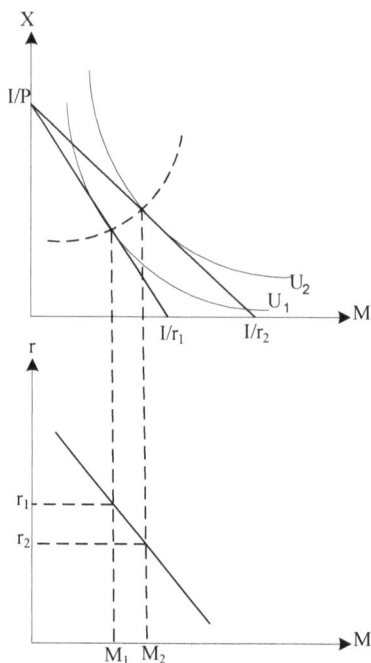

Figure 2-6: The curve for the nominal demand for money function

An individual will normally have to repay less money for the interest rate in such situations. This money could be used in purchasing larger deals of substitute commodities while a larger sum of money could be kept by the individual. Therefore, the lower interest rate prompts keeping more money and increased demands for money and as the figure shows, money demand function will develop a descending slope. However, it should be noted that this is a nominal demand for money function, i.e., this function has been developed in $r, M/P$ setting. To draw the real demand for money function, we first acquire the money function in $r, M/P$ setting. For this, we have to divide the budget constraint function on P:

$$\frac{I}{P} = r.\frac{M}{P} + P.\frac{X}{P}$$

If M=0, then $X = \dfrac{I}{P}$ and if X=0, then $\dfrac{M}{P} = \dfrac{I}{r.P}$ . Therefore, the real demand for money function could be drawn in r,M/P setting.

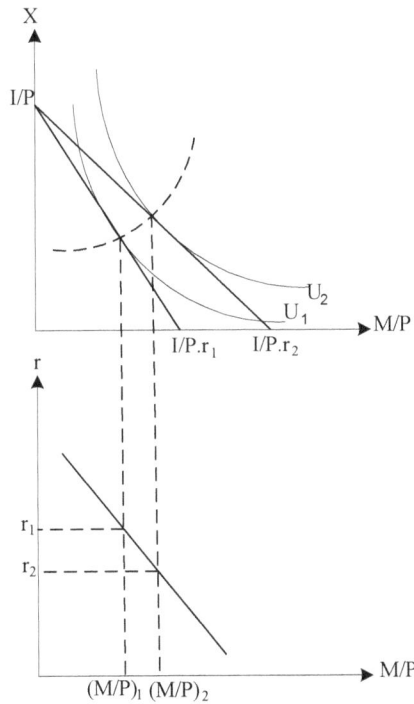

Figure 2-7: The curve for the real demand for money function

As the figure suggests, lowering the interest rate has pushed the budget constraint to the right and has given the individual a basket characterized with stronger total utility. Now the individual could keep more money (M) and thus more M/P. The graph clearly demonstrates that lowered interest rate prompts increases in demands for real money balance. We could extract the curve for money demands which indicates the inverse relationship between money demands and the interest rates.

It should be noted that the demand displayed in the previous figure is just a certain mode of money demand function. For example, there are three more other types given below:

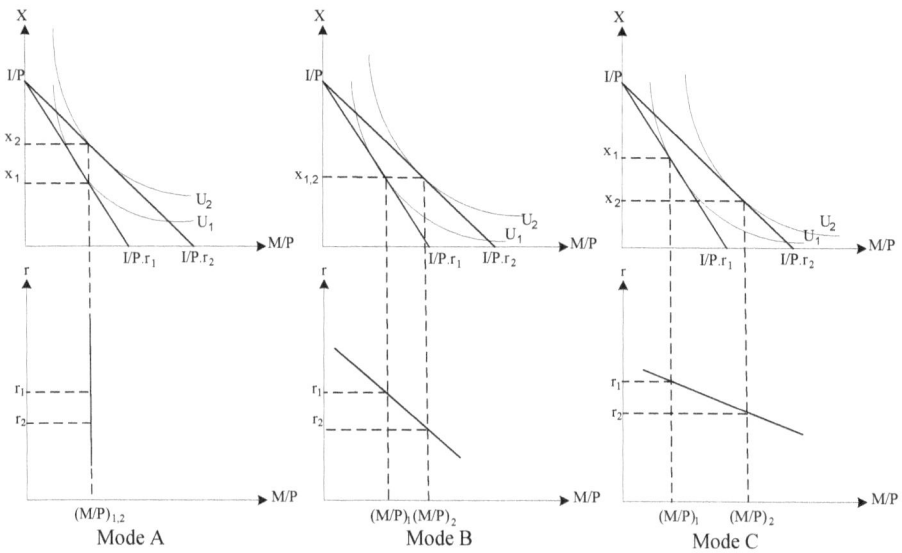

Figure 2-8: Different types of curves of the real demand for money function

Mode A shows money with zero elasticity, Mode B shows money with consistent elasticity while mode C with higher elasticity. Mode A is very important here where the substitution and income effects are equal yet are in the reverse direction. Therefore, the whole extra money acquired as a result of lowering the interest rate is spent on substitute commodities and there is no change in the balance of real money. Thus the balance of real money is not vulnerable to the interest rate. Technically speaking, the vulnerability of money demands to the interest rate is zero and the money is inelastic.

So far, we have extracted the graphic function of the money demand function in which the balance of real money was indirectly related to the interest rate. We attempt to figure out the related equations.

## - Extracting the equation for money demand function

To extract the money demand function, we will follow the previous procedures. So far, we have found that people with limited funds seek to maximize their overall utility, which refers to the sum of the acquired utility from money and money substitutes. Therefore, the above problem can be illustrated as follows:

$$\text{MAX } U = \int u(X,M).e^{-pt}\, dt$$

$$I = r.M + p.X$$

The above problem is one of the familiar issues in economics and can be used by different methods, one of which is to form the Lagrange function:

$$L = U(M,X) + \lambda[I - r.M - p.X]$$

After the formation of the Lagrange function and the derivation of the first order conditions, we will have:

$$\frac{\partial L}{\partial M} = \frac{\partial U}{\partial M} - \lambda.r = 0 \rightarrow \frac{\partial U}{\partial M} = \lambda.r$$

$$\frac{\partial L}{\partial X} = \frac{\partial U}{\partial X} - \lambda.p = 0 \rightarrow \frac{\partial U}{\partial X} = \lambda.p$$

By dividing the two expressions, we will have:

$$\frac{MU_M}{MU_X} = \frac{r}{p} \rightarrow \frac{MU_M}{r} = \frac{MU_X}{p}$$

The graphical form of the above equations presented earlier shows that the equilibrium condition and the optimum point are located at a point where the slope of the equal utility curve is equal to that of the budget constraint curve. Similarly, as it was noted earlier, the relative monetary utility should be equal to the final utility of its alternative goods.

Focusing on the marginal monetary utility, in the first section of this chapter we have shown that the marginal monetary utility has an inverse relationship with money supply, in a way that as money supply (M) increases the marginal monetary utility ($MU_M$) will decrease. Although this basic rule is absolutely correct, that function was plotted for an individual so that the marginal monetary utility is the inverse function of the amount of cash held:

$$MU_M = B.\frac{1}{M}$$

Where, $B$ is constant. Now, we want to generalize this relationship to the society. The marginal monetary utility in the whole society is equal to the final utility of the average of each individual in the society. Therefore, the average utility of the community should be calculated. Since the marginal utility of each individual is inversely associated with their average money supply and that the average money supply for each individual is equal to the total money supply in the society divided by the number of people living in it, thus the marginal monetary utility for the whole society is inversely related to per capita money supply, where N in the following equation stands for the population:

$$MU_M = B.\frac{1}{M/N}$$

But this relationship is not yet complete and needs to be improved because the marginal monetary utility varies from one person to another and it depends on their productivity. Therefore, in order to calculate the average marginal utility for each person, the number of people should be multiplied by the productive of any person (N.A):

$$MU_M = B.\frac{1}{M/A.N}$$

Of course, one of the best indicators of productivity is per capita production (y). So by multiplying the number of people in their per capita production (N.y), it can be suggested that the marginal monetary utility is an inverse function of the effective per capita money supply in the society:

$$MU_M = B . \dfrac{1}{M\big/N.y}$$

On the other hand, previously we had:

$$\dfrac{MU_M}{r} = \dfrac{MU_X}{p} \rightarrow MU_M = \dfrac{r.MU_X}{p}$$

Now, by replacing the average marginal monetary utility of the society in the above equation, we will have:

$$B . \dfrac{1}{M\big/N.y} = \dfrac{r.MU_X}{p}$$

Simplifying the above equation, the monetary demand function will be obtained:

$$\dfrac{M}{p} = \dfrac{B}{MU_X} . \dfrac{1}{r} . N.y$$

As the monetary demand function indicates, per capita production and population are directly related to money demand, so that as the per capita production increases, the demand for money will also increase. Similarly, as the population grows, demand for money will also increase. On the other hand, the interest rate has an indirect relationship with the demand for money. This inverse relationship has already been shown in graphical form.

In addition, it is clear that if the number of people (N) is multiplied by the per capita production (y), it yields the total production for the society (Y). Therefore, N.y can be replaced by Y in the monetary demand equation:

$$\frac{M}{p} = (\frac{B}{MU_X}) . \frac{Y}{r}$$

Therefore, as it is clear from the obtained function, demand for money is directly related to income and indirectly related to the interest rate, so that as the income level increases, the demand for money will increase, while as interest rates increases, the demand for money will decrease.

On the other hand B is a constant that by an increase in its value will increase the demand for money. In addition, the demand for money is inversely related to the marginal utility of the money substitute, so that the higher the marginal utility of the money substitute, the lower will be the demand for money.

As it was shown earlier, the money demand curve is a downward curve, and according to the above equation, we know that the money demand curve is downward and nonlinear in terms of the interest rate.

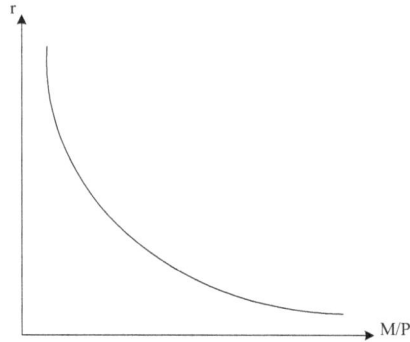

Figure 2.9: Nonlinear curve of the real money demand function

If the following value is shown by K:

$$K = \frac{B}{MU_X} \cdot \frac{1}{r}$$

In other words, if K is function of B, r, and $MU_X$, then the money demand function can be rewritten as follows:

$$\frac{M}{p} = K(B, MU_X, r).Y \rightarrow \frac{M}{p} = K.Y$$

This form of money demand function suggests that money demand is a coefficient (K) of the income, which in turn stresses the significance of multiple theories of the demand for money.

In this function, like the demand functions proposed by Ricardo, Fisher, Marshall, and others, the demand for money depends on income, and the main difference is that the coefficient (K) is not constant and is influenced by variables B, r, and $MU_X$.

Since in addition to the direct impact of income on money demand, the interest rate has an adverse effect on it, so this function highlights the Keynesian theory of money demand. The difference is that unlike the Keynesian theory of money demand, here the transaction, precautionary, and speculative demands for money are not separated and all are aggregated in the form demand for money. Thus, as was previously noted, instead of considering three motives for money demand, people asking for money only under the influence of their "comfort motive". In other words, contrary to Keynes' view, people not divide their money into three transaction, precautionary, and speculative parts. For example, when interest rates raise it is not only the speculative money demand that decreases but also a person will decrease his total demand for money, even transactional, precautionary or any real money balance without differencing between his own real money balances.

This money demand function, such as Tobin's demand for money, suggests a reverse impact of the interest rate on the total demand for money, not just the speculative demand for money. Also, this money demand function, like Bamol and Tobin's theory, suggests that money demand is directly related to income, and indirectly to the interest rate, but this is true for the total demand for money not just the transactional demand for money.

In addition, similar to Friedman's theory of demand for money, this money demand function suggests that income has a positive effect on the demand for money and the interest rate through its effect on coefficient K has an inverse relationship with the demand for money. However, this function has strong rational foundations on one hand and on the other hand it is not the interest rate that affects K, but also it is derived by the marginal utility of all money substitutes. As a result, it is clear that the obtained money demand function supports the previous theories but it presents a more complete version of such theories.

**- The slope of money demand function**

We so far have extracted the money demand function and have drawn its graph. Now it's time to compute and interpret the slope of the money demand function. As the acquired relationship shows, this slope is negative and descending.

$$\frac{\partial r}{\partial \frac{M}{P}} = \frac{-B}{MU_X} \cdot \frac{1}{(\frac{M}{P})^2} \cdot Y$$

As it is clear, the slope of the money demands is inversely related to the money mass yet directly associated with the income. On the other hand, the stronger the marginal utility of the money substitutes, the less steep the slope of the money demand function. In addition, money demands are much less vulnerable to the interest rate. The least variations in the interest rate (and consequently the demands for money substitutes) bring about greater changes in the money demands.

We will address the special modes of the slope of money demands.

## - Horizontal money demand function:

For the money demand function to be horizontal, these conditions must be met:

$$\frac{\partial r}{\partial \frac{M}{P}} = 0 \text{ and } \frac{\partial \frac{M}{P}}{\partial r} = \infty$$

$$\frac{\partial r}{\partial \frac{M}{P}} = 0 \rightarrow \lim_{\frac{M}{P} \to \infty} \frac{-B}{MU_X} \cdot \frac{1}{(\frac{M}{P})^2} . Y = 0$$

$$\frac{\partial \frac{M}{P}}{\partial r} = \infty \rightarrow \lim_{r \to 0} \frac{-B}{MU_X} \cdot \frac{1}{(r)^2} . Y = \infty$$

Moreover, $\frac{\partial r}{\partial M / P}$ will be zero if $\frac{M}{P}$ tends to infinity, i.e. when the money demand is very large. In addition, $\frac{\partial M / P}{\partial r}$ will be indefinite if only r tends to zero or when the profit rate is very low. Therefore, large money demands $\frac{M}{P} \to \infty$ and low interest rates s are two characteristics of horizontal money demand functions.

This characteristic has already been specified in the lower part (part A) of the money demand function where money demand ( $\frac{M}{P}$ ) is very high while the interest rate is very low and thus the slope in this function is very small.

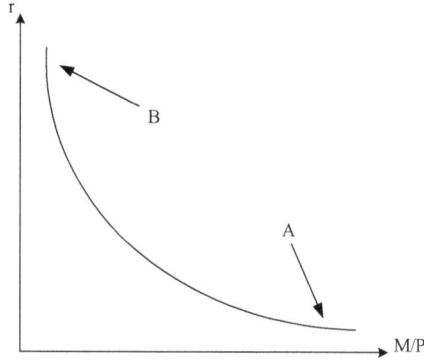

Figure 10-2: Horizontal and vertical components of the curve of real demand for money function

**-Vertical money demand function:**

$\dfrac{\partial r}{\partial \dfrac{M}{P}} = \infty$ and $\dfrac{\partial \dfrac{M}{P}}{\partial r} = 0$ must be in place if we want the curve of the money demand function to be vertical.

$$\frac{\partial r}{\partial \frac{M}{P}} = \infty \to \lim_{\frac{M}{P} \to 0} \frac{-B}{MU_X} \cdot \frac{1}{(\frac{M}{P})^2} . Y = \infty$$

$$\frac{\partial \frac{M}{P}}{\partial r} = 0 \to \lim_{r \to \infty} \frac{-B}{MU_X} \cdot \frac{1}{(r)^2} . Y = 0$$

Given the constancy of other variables, $\dfrac{\partial r}{\partial M / P}$ will be indefinite if only $\dfrac{M}{P}$ tends to zero, e.i. when the demand for money is very low.

On the other hand, $\dfrac{\partial M/P}{\partial r}$ will be zero if only r tends to zero e.i. when the interest rate is very large. Therefore, low money demands $\dfrac{M}{P} \to 0$ and high interest rates $r \to \infty$ are two characteristics of the vertical money demand function .

This characteristic has already been specified in the upper part (part B) of the money demand function where money demand ($\dfrac{M}{P}$) is very low while the interest rate is very high and thus the slope in this function is very large.

In general, two old and new money demand functions could be compared:

$$\dfrac{M}{p} = KY - hr$$

$$\dfrac{M}{p} = \dfrac{B}{MU_x} \cdot \dfrac{1}{r} \cdot Y$$

When there is no income in the old money demand function (Y=0), there is still demands for money ($\dfrac{M}{p} = -hr$). In contrast, there is no demand for money ($\dfrac{M}{p} = 0$) in the new function if there is no income (Y=0).

On the other hand, sensitivity of the money to the income was always constant and equal to K in the old version of money demand function while there are variable sensitivity levels to the income in the new version. Demands for money, in particular, are inversely related to the interest rate i.e. higher interest rates mean lower sensitivity of the money to the income.

$$\frac{\partial \frac{M}{P}}{\partial Y} = \frac{1}{K}$$

$$\frac{\partial \frac{M}{P}}{\partial Y} = \frac{B}{MU_X} \cdot \frac{1}{r}$$

In addition, while the sensitivity of money demands to interest rates are only dependent on h value in the old function; it depends on four factors in the new version. Higher the incomes, more sensitivity money demands are to the interest rates. Furthermore, when the interest rates are low, the sensitivity of money demands is higher.

$$\frac{\partial \frac{M}{P}}{\partial r} = -h$$

$$\frac{\partial \frac{M}{P}}{\partial r} = \frac{-B}{MU_X} \cdot \frac{Y}{(r)^2}$$

**-Money Market Equilibrium**

We extracted both money demands function and graph in the previous part. Now we look into the money market balance in this section. To keep matters simple, the money demand function is considered exogenous and independent of the interest rate:

$$\frac{M^D}{p} = (\frac{B}{MU_X}).\frac{1}{r}.Y$$

$$\frac{M^S}{p} = \frac{M}{p}$$

As the figure shows, when the interest rate is $r_0$ and the income is $Y_0$, money demand and supply are equal at **a** point and thus the money market is in equilibrium. However, if the income increases, the money demand function moves to the right of the graph. Thus the former interest rate propelled extra demands for money. However, in cases of fixed money volumes, the interest rate increases in order to decrease extra money demands and restore the equilibrium of the money market. The new B point corresponds to b with $r_1, Y_1$ coordinates. Therefore, all the produced points correspond to the equilibrium of the money market at r,Y coordinates. This curve is the same as the money market equilibrium or LM.

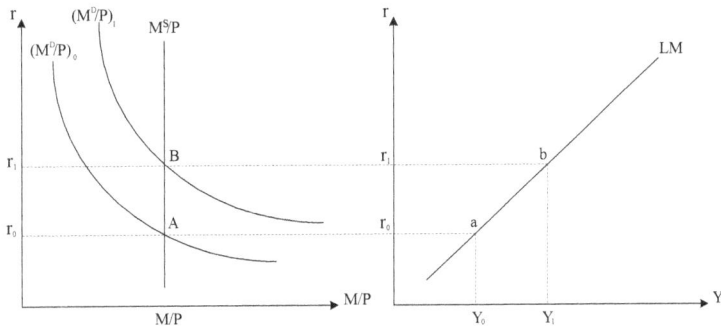

Figure 11.2: Money Market Equilibrium Curve

Given the acquired relations, the LM function is worked out as follows from the equilibrium of the money market:

$$\frac{M^D}{p} = \frac{M^S}{p} \rightarrow \frac{M^D}{p} = (\frac{B}{MU_X}).\frac{1}{r}.Y \rightarrow r = (\frac{B}{MU_X}).\frac{1}{\frac{M}{p}}.Y$$

This function sums all the geometrical points of the interest rate r and the income (Y) where money demands equal its supply and the money market is in equilibrium. As the figure and the function clearly show, the income and the interest rate are directly related. In other words, higher interest rates bring about increased incomes to keep the money market in equilibrium. The slope $\frac{\partial r}{\partial Y}$ of LM function could be computed as follows:

$$\frac{\partial r}{\partial Y} = \frac{B}{MU_X}.\frac{1}{\frac{M}{p}}$$

As it is obvious, bigger B variable and smaller Mux give rise to a sharper LM slope. On the other hand, increased money volume, $\frac{M}{P}$ prompts money demand function to develop a slanted slope.

We now study the special modes of LM curve.

**-Horizontal LM Curve**

Given the slope of the LM curve, in cases of large money volumes ( $\frac{M}{P} \rightarrow \infty$ ), LM curve will be horizontal.

$$\frac{\partial r}{\partial Y} = 0 \to \lim \frac{B}{MU_x} \cdot \frac{1}{\left(\frac{M}{P}\right)} = 0$$

However, considering the function of LM curve, whenever $\frac{M}{P}$ tends to infinity, the interest rate tends to zero. We have already seen that $\frac{M}{P} \to \infty, r \to 0$ are two characteristics of the horizontal money demand function. Thus this function will be followed by horizontal LM curve.

Horizontal LM curve is termed "liquidity trap" and now we can prove two important characteristics of this trap. Liquidity trap could then be defined as cases where money demands are large ($\frac{M}{P} \to \infty$) while the interest rate is very small ($r \to 0$).

### -Vertical LM Curve

Given the slope of LM curve, whenever $\frac{M}{P}$ tends to zero, LM will follow a vertical pattern. We have already learned that decreases in $\frac{M}{P}$ results in higher interest rates r and thus $\frac{M}{P} \to 0, r \to \infty$ are two characteristics of the vertical LM function.

### -The efficiency of monetary policies

Monetary policies are one of major responses of economic decision-makers of every country to varying economic scenarios. The efficiency of monetary policies are defined as changes in the income

(dY) per each change in the money volume $\frac{M}{P}$ and therefore, larger

the $\frac{\partial Y}{\partial \frac{M}{P}}$, higher the efficiency of these policies.

This relation was in form of $\frac{1}{K}$ in the old version of LM function.

Since K is a constant value, monetary policies evenly affect different interest rates. Higher volumes of money will move the LM function in parallels to the right:

$$LM : r = -\frac{M}{P}\frac{1}{h} + \frac{K}{h}Y \rightarrow \frac{\partial Y}{\partial \frac{M}{P}} = \frac{1}{K}$$

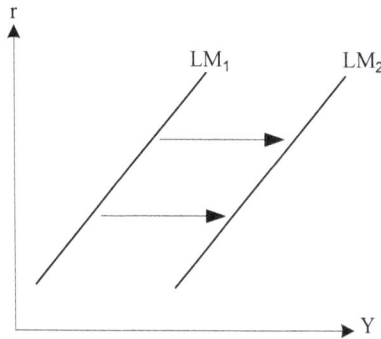

Figure 12-2: The efficiency of monetary policies in the old version of LM curve

However, the efficiency of monetary policies is computed as below in the new version of LM curve:

$$LM : r = \frac{B}{MU_X} \cdot \frac{1}{(\frac{M}{P})} \cdot Y \rightarrow \frac{\partial Y}{\partial \frac{M}{P}} = r \cdot \frac{MU_X}{B}$$

As it is obvious, the efficiency of monetary policies is dependent are three factors of B, r and Mux. If we assume $\lambda = \frac{MU_X}{B}$ to be constant, then:

$$\frac{\partial Y}{\partial \frac{M}{P}} = \lambda \cdot r$$

In other words, the monetary policies are dependent on the interest rate. Therefore, countries implementing higher interest rates could practice these policies in better ways. In addition, since the horizontal transfer or the LM depends on the interest rate, the LM curve moves to right in a non-parallel mode which is in contrast to the its old mode. This means that the adoption of monetary policies at higher interest rates causes stronger horizontal transference of Y while lowering the interest rates constrains the abilities of Y, resulting in weaker transference of the LM curve.

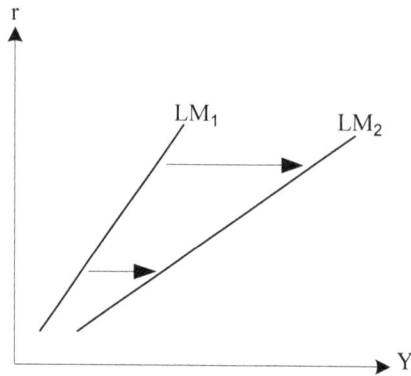

Figure 13-2: The efficiency of monetary policies in the new version

of LM curve

It should be noted that considering the previous definition of

$K = \dfrac{B}{MU_X} \cdot \dfrac{1}{r}$, monetary policies are still $\dfrac{1}{K}$ in both new and old

versions of the LM curve in terms of efficiency. However, the new

curve is more comprehensive.

$$\frac{\partial Y}{\partial \dfrac{M}{P}} = r \cdot \frac{MU_X}{B} = \frac{1}{k}$$

## - The consumer equilibrium and the quantity theory of money

Quantity theory of money is one of the most basic economic

equations whose changes over time can reveal the evolution of the

ideas of economics. This theory with all its criticisms and

modifications through its history is considered as one of the most

fundamental equations in economics which has survived the

controversies of many thinkers for more than three centuries and is one of the theories with the highest level of consensus and the slightest changes throughout its history. However, despite its importance and its significant place in the analysis of economics, this theory not been based on a solid foundation and has often been accepted as an intuitive equation. So, in the following sections, we try to use the principles of microeconomics to provide a solid foundation for quantity theory of money, to prove it, and by elaborating and expanding it shed light on its ambiguous aspects and achieve new results. Besides, we seek to extract important applied policies from this theory to advance economy.

We start our discussion by focusing on maximizing utility by the representative household. The household seeks to maximize its utility (by having money and money substitutes) in lieu of existing costs (the opportunity cost of lost money and the cost of acquiring money substitutes).

Substituting this equation in the formula used for calculating p, we have:

$$p = r.MU_X . \frac{1}{B. \frac{1}{M/N.y}}$$

Rearranging the above equation, we will have:

$$p = r.MU_X . \frac{1}{B} . \frac{M}{N.y}$$

V function can be defined as follows:

$$V = V(r, MU_X, \frac{1}{B})$$

Now, we will have:

$$p = V(r, MU_X, \frac{1}{B}) \cdot \frac{M}{N.y}$$

On the other hand, we know that per capita production (y) multiplied by the population (N) yields total production (Y = N.y). Replacing it in the above equation and rearranging it, we will have:

$$M.V(r, MU_X, \frac{1}{B}) = P.Y$$

As it can be seen, the obtained equation is in effect the same as quantity theory of money:

$$M.V = P.Y$$

Therefore, we managed to extract the quantity theory of money by maximizing the utility of the representative household. Of course, this equation can also be written:

$$M = \frac{1}{V(r, MU_X, \frac{1}{B})} \cdot P.Y$$

By substituting K = 1/V, we have:

$$\frac{M}{P} = K(r, MU_X, \frac{1}{B}).Y$$

The above equation is the same as the money demand function we had previously obtained.

The first point to note is that the calculated V (and K) is not a fixed value and is influenced by three factors r, B, and $MU_X$. Therefore, as the marginal utility of money substitutes increase, the demand for them also increases but it decreases when velocity of money (V) increases or coefficient K decreases. On the other hand, by increasing the interest rate r, the lost opportunity cost increases, so with increasing velocity V or decreasing K, the demand for money will decrease.

Secondly, by substituting the multiplication of population and per capita production (Ny) instead of total production (Y), we will have:

$$\frac{M}{P} = K.N.y$$

Therefore, as the population grows, first, the demand for money will increase, and second, in accordance with ceteris paribus assumption, with increasing population, prices will decrease. This result will be described in greater detail later.

In sum, as the population and productivity increase, the demand for money will also increase. The population growth increases the demand for money in two ways. First, by increasing the number of people demanding money, and second by increasing the total production and the need for trading these products, more money is demanded. Productivity also increases the demand for money in two ways. First, people with higher productivity demand more money as in return for their pay or salary, so the demand for money increases. Second, as productivity increases, production will also increase and since supplying goods entails the demand for money, then the higher supply of goods will raise the demand for money. As a result, with the increasing population and productivity, the demand for money (M/P) will increase, and if the money supply (M) is constant, the prices (P) decrease.

These issues could be observed in the following graph.

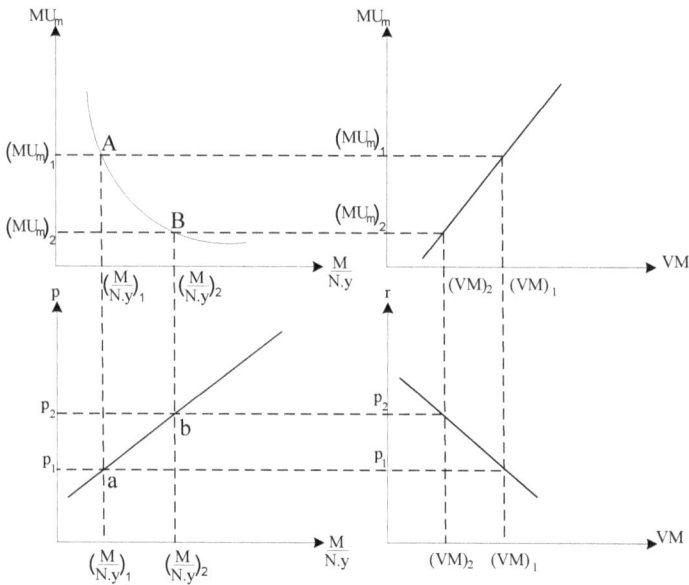

Figure 14-2: The effects of effective per-capita money on general prices

60

The left part of this graph shows how effective per-capita money and the marginal utility of money are related based on $MU_M = B.\dfrac{1}{M \Big/ N.y}$ while the right part indicates that prices go up more the money loses its value. We start from the point A on the upper graph which is on the left side of the figure, then continue with the effective initial volume of money to reach P1 price on the lower graph which is on the left side of the graph in the point a.

Now, if the effective per capita money is raised (volumes of money increase or the population or per capita decreases), as suggested in the graph above, the marginal money utility decreases. It can be seen on the right side of the graph that decreased marginal money lowers the money value which in turn leads to higher prices (right upper part of the graph). This trend guides to the b point on the left lower part of the graph i.e. increases in prices.

Through this process, we came up with ab curve which reveals a direct relation between the volumes of effective per capita money and prices which is already indicated in this relation:

$$P = V.\frac{M}{N.y}$$

This above relation is in fact the formula for the lower left curve (ab). Thus the slope of this graph is the same as velocity of money flows:

$$\frac{\partial P}{\partial \dfrac{M}{N.y}} = V(r, MU_X, \frac{1}{B})$$

Therefore, higher the velocity of money, more drastic will be the effects of changes of in the volumes of effective per capita money on the prices.

As already shown, the productivity was replaced with per capita production to help the readers better understand the basic concepts (based on the old quantity theory of money).However, we now rewrite the relations using the productivity variable (A) to extract some important results:

$$\text{MAX } U = \int u(X, M). e^{-pt} \, dt$$

$$I = r.M + p.X$$

We form a Lagrange function to solve this question:

$$L = U(M, X) + \lambda \left[ I - r.M - p.X \right]$$

Once Lagrange function has been formed and first order derivatives are calculated:

$$\frac{\partial L}{\partial M} = \frac{\partial U}{\partial M} - \lambda.r = 0 \rightarrow MU_M = \lambda.r$$

$$\frac{\partial L}{\partial X} = \frac{\partial U}{\partial X} - \lambda.p = 0 \rightarrow MU_X = \lambda.p$$

$$\frac{MU_M}{MU_X} = \frac{r}{p} \rightarrow \frac{MU_M}{r} = \frac{MU_X}{p} \rightarrow p = r.MU_X.\frac{1}{MU_M}$$

As previously shown, money marginal utility is inversely related to the volumes of effective per capita money:

$$MU_M = B.\dfrac{1}{M\diagup N.A}$$

We will arrive at the relation below after considering the marginal money utility and simplifying the formula:

$$p = V(r, MU_X, \dfrac{1}{B}).\dfrac{M}{N.A}$$

Calculating a logarithm for both sides produces the following equation:

$$LN(P) = LN(V) + LN(M) - LN(N) - LN(A)$$

Calculation of derivatives will give the following relation:

$$\dfrac{\partial P}{P} = \dfrac{\partial V}{V} + \dfrac{\partial M}{M} - \dfrac{\partial N}{N} - \dfrac{\partial A}{A}$$

Since changes of a variable will produce its growth once divided on that variable, we come to:

$$\dot{P} = \dot{V} + \dot{M} - \dot{N} - \dot{A}$$

This relation is a crucial one because it shows that increases in the velocity of money as well as the volumes of money will result into higher prices while increased population and improved productivity brings the prices down. For purpose of simplicity and ease of analysis, let's assume that money flows have a fixed velocity or V=0. We thus arrive at:

$$\dot{P} = \dot{M} - (\dot{N} + \dot{A})$$

Now if we wish to bring the changes in prices i.e. inflation to zero, we must:

$$\dot{P} = 0 \rightarrow \dot{M} = (\dot{N} + \dot{A})$$

The following general rule could be developed for optimal money growth:

**"The optimal money growth is the sum of population growth and the growth of productivity"**

Therefore, the growth of the volumes of money must equal the growth of both the population and the productivity to prevent changes in the marginal money utility and the prices. Considering the significance of the argument and to better understand the point raised, we follow up the issue in form of P number (B is assigned 10 in all the modes):

We first concentrate on the population. The table 2.1 shows the first mode (the first row) of the new quantity theory of money

$$M.V(r, MU_X, \frac{1}{B}) = P.(N.y)$$

.

Table 1.2: Changes in the volumes of money and the population

| Y | N | M/Ny | MU$_M$ | M | V | P | Y= N.y |
|---|---|---|---|---|---|---|---|
| 10 | 10 | 1 | 10 | 100 | 2 | 2 | 10×100=10 |
| 10 | 100 | 0.1 | 100 | 100 | 2 | 0.2 | 10×1000=100 |
| 10 | 100 | 1 | 10 | 1000 | 2 | 2 | 10×1000=100 |

If only the population increases yet the productivity and the volumes of money stay the same, the volumes of effective per capita will drop. As a result and considering the equation:

$$MU_M = B.\frac{1}{M/N.A}$$, the marginal money utility will increase which in

turn decreases the prices to restore balance to the quantity theory of money. In the next mode of the initial status (the first row), both the population and accordingly the volumes of the money have grown (the third row). This does not bring about any changes in the volumes of effective per capita money and thus money marginal utility

$$MU_M = B.\frac{1}{M/N.A}$$ and the prices will not undergo changes. Due to the

fact that the total production and the population increase on the right side of the quantity theory of money as a result of increases in the volumes of the money on the left side of it, this theory will be established again if increases in the population and the volumes of money are in proportion (provided that there is no change in the levels of prices).


This is also true for the productivity growth.

Table 2.2: Changes in the volumes of money and the productivity

| y | N | M/Ny | MU$_M$ | M | V | P | Y= N.y |
|---|---|---|---|---|---|---|---|
| 10 | 10 | 1 | 10 | 100 | 2 | 2 | 10×100=10 |
| 100 | 10 | 0.1 | 100 | 100 | 2 | 0.2 | 10×1000=100 |
| 100 | 10 | 1 | 10 | 1000 | 2 | 2 | 10×1000=100 |

Compared to the first row, only productivity has increased in the second row. Therefore, according to $MU_M = B.\dfrac{1}{M/_{N.A}}$, marginal money utility goes down and consequently prices decrease to allow for the reestablishment of the quantity theory of the money. If other variables stay stable and the volumes of the money increase in proportion to the increases in the productivity, prices will stay the same and the theory will be still in play.

We assume in the last example that both variables of productivity and population increase:

Table 3.2: Changes in the volumes of money, population and the productivity

| y | N | M/Ny | MU$_M$ | M | V | P | Y= N.y |
|---|---|---|---|---|---|---|---|
| 10 | 10 | 1 | 10 | 100 | 2 | 2 | 10×100=10 |
| 100 | 100 | 0.01 | 1000 | 100 | 2 | 0.02 | 100×10000=100 |
| 100 | 100 | 1 | 10 | 10000 | 2 | 2 | 100×10000=100 |
| 100 | 100 | 10 | 1 | 100000 | 2 | 20 | 100×10000=100 |

If other variables stay fixed (in particular the volumes of the money) and only productivity and population grow (the second row), prices will go down to allow the theory to be still in play. In contrast, if the volumes of the money increase in proportion to the sums of increases of productivity and population (the third row) i.e. if M= (N+A), then the the quantity theory of the money will be still in force and prices will not have any change s (P=0). However, prices will go up if the increases in the volumes of the money surpass those of population and productivity (the fourth row).

Based on the equation of the marginal utility money, the afore-mentioned example and the previous essential principle, we can assert that the marginal money utility must be controlled to avoid fluctuations in the prices. If we develop a logarithm from the marginal money utility:

$$MU_M = B.\frac{1}{M/N.A}$$

$$MU_M = B.\frac{1}{M/N.A} \rightarrow LN(MU_M) = LN(B) - \left[LN(M) - LN(N) - LN(A)\right]$$

We come to this after differentiation:

$$\dot{MU}_M = \dot{B} - \left[\dot{M} - (\dot{N} + \dot{A})\right]$$

Since B is a constant number and zero changes (B=0), we have:

$$\dot{MU}_M = -\left[\dot{M} - (\dot{N} + \dot{A})\right]$$

How much marginal money utility $\dot{MU}_M \downarrow$ decreases depends on how big the gap is between the growth of the volumes of the money (M) and the sums of the growths observed in both productivity and population (N+A). If we thus wish to keep marginal money utility stable $\dot{MU}_M = 0$, variations of the volumes of the money must be in proportion to the sums of changes in both productivity and population:

$$\dot{MU}_M = 0 \rightarrow \dot{M} = \dot{N} + \dot{A}$$

Prices will stay the same in this scenario (P=0) which is crucial. If we wish to keep the general prices fixed and prevent the development of inflation, we must increase the volumes of the money equal to the sums of the increases of both productivity and population which leads us to this basic principle:

**"The money marginal utility must be stable if the stability of prices is desired"**

**"The volumes of the money must increase in proportion to the sums of the increases of both productivity and population if the stability of the money marginal utility is targeted"**

In other words, prices will go up in proportion to the difference between the growth of the volumes of the money and the sums of the growths observed in both productivity and population. In fact, prices depend in the money marginal utility. Therefore, the bigger the drop in the money marginal utility, the easier it becomes for the individual to part with their money and thus the individual is much more willing to pay money in exchange for a certain commodity which ultimately increases then prices.[1]

---

[1] - Let's assume that the marginal utility of money-substitute commodities and the volume of production don't undergo any changes ($\dot{Y} = \dot{MU}_x = 0$). Here, for example, a 10% increase in the money volume brings about a 10% drop in the money marginal utility which gives us:

$$\frac{MU_m}{r} < \frac{MU_x}{p}$$

Therefore, for restoration of the balance to occur, either prices ($\dot{p}$) must go up by 10% or the interest rate ($\dot{r}$) must go down by 10% or a combination of both. In other words, ($\dot{P} - \dot{r}$) must go up by 10%. These results could be shown in another way. According to the quantity theory of money:

$$M.V(r, MU_x) = P.Y$$

If we have full-employment status and assume that the money volume increases:

$$M.V(r, MU_x) > P.Y$$

Then on one hand the prices go up as result of increased money volume to enlarge the phrase on the right side of the relation while the interest rate goes down on the other hand to slow down the money velocity. Therefore, a combination of increased prices and lower interest rate restore the balance.

If B=1, then the quantity theory of money could be re-written as follows:

$$M.r.MU_x = P.Y$$

If we develop logarithms from two sides of the relation and then obtain derivatives for them:

$$\dot{M} + \dot{r} + \dot{MU}_x = \dot{P} + \dot{Y}$$

If we assume that the variations of the marginal utility of money-substitute commodities and the production changes are zero ($\dot{Y} = \dot{MU}_x = 0$) then we have:

$$\dot{M} = (\dot{P} - \dot{r})$$

We then come to the following general rule:

**Assuming the constancy of the marginal utility of money-substitute commodities as well as the production, increases in both the prices and the interest rate ($\dot{P} - \dot{r}$) will do take place in proportion to the growth of money volume ($\dot{M}$).**

## - Producer equilibrium and quantity theory of money

By examining consumer behavior, we tried to build microeconomic foundations for quantity theory of money. Consider a representative household that seeks to maximize its utility given its budget constraints. In this way, we build microeconomic foundations for quantity theory of money and then calculate the optimal money growth.

Here we focus on the producer behavior. In fact, in the previous section, we considered a typical consumer who seeks to maximize his/her utility. Now, we consider a typical producer who seeks to maximize his/her profit.

For the sake of simplicity, we assume that the producer faces only labor costs. Therefore, the producer's goal is to maximize the total value of discounted profits of different time periods:

$$MAX\pi = \int (P.F(N) - w.N)e^{-rt}dt$$

In the above equation, P.F(N) represents the amount of revenue generated by the sale of goods and w.N donates the cost of the firm (related to labor). So, $\pi$ represents the difference between income and expenditure that is profit. In order to obtain optimal values, we have to take the derivative from the profit equation and get the resulting expression equal to zero.

$$\frac{\partial \pi}{\partial N} = P.F'(N) - w = 0$$

So we will have:

$$P.F'(N) = w \rightarrow P = \frac{w}{F'(N)}$$

The numerator and denominator of the fraction on the right are multiplied by N:

$$P = \frac{w}{F'(N)} \cdot \frac{N}{N}$$

The numerator of the above fraction is the same of total wage of labor denoted by W:

$$P = \frac{W}{N.F'(N)}$$

The term F'(N) is the marginal product of labor ($MP_N$):

$$P = \frac{W}{N.MP_N}$$

The marginal product of labor ($MP_N$) is an indicator of productivity (A):

$$P = \frac{W}{N.A}$$

On the other hand, the total wage of labor is paid by money, and a portion of the wage is paid every time money is handed over. Thus, it can be suggested that the money supply multiplied by the velocity of money is equal to the total wage of labor, that means:

$$W = V.M$$

By replacing this equation in the previous one, we will have:

$$P = \frac{V.M}{N.A}$$

For the sake of simplicity, we take per capita production as a substitute for productivity:

$$P = \frac{V.M}{N.y}$$

On the other hand, we know the number of people (N) multiplied by per capita production (y) is equal to total production (Y):

$$N.y = Y$$

By replacing this equation in the previous one, we will have:

$$P = \frac{V.M}{Y} \rightarrow M.V = P.Y$$

This is the same as quantity theory of money. So, with the maximization of producer profits, we were able to redefine quantity theory of money in terms of microeconomic foundations.

Previously, to prove quantity theory of money, we used per capita production (y) instead of productivity (A). But now we have:

$$P = \frac{V.M}{N.A}$$

By taking the logarithms of the two sides of the equation, we will have:

$$LN(P) = LN(V) + LN(M) - LN(N) - LN(A)$$

We now take the derivatives of both sides:

$$\frac{\partial P}{P} = \frac{\partial V}{V} + \frac{\partial M}{M} - \frac{\partial N}{N} - \frac{\partial A}{A}$$

From the definition of growth, we will have:

$$\dot{P} = \dot{V} + \dot{M} - \dot{N} - \dot{A}$$

If we take the velocity of money fixed ($V' = 0$), in order not to have inflation ($P' = 0$), the optimal growth of money will be equal to the sum of population growth and productivity growth:

$$\dot{M} = \dot{N} + \dot{A}$$

This is the same result we previously achieved by maximizing the consumer utility, and now we did the same by maximizing the profit of the representative firm.

## - The Laws of Motion of Money

Centuries ago scientists and thinkers sought to know the laws governing the motion of bojects. This is even apparent in the books of thinkers tens of centuries ago, such as Aristotle and Plato. Scientists have sought to know that what laws is followed by motion of objects. These discussions followed a dramatic advance after Isaac Newton.

Newton carried out a lot of studies on the motion of objects and found three rules in this regard.

These three Newton motion laws transformed our perspective on the motion of objects in general, and helped us recognize the type of motion of bodies.

We are here trying to extract the lows of motion for an economic commodity called "money".Money and its motion are fundamentally different from other objects and commodities. We will outline the laws of the motion of money.

**Law 1: If a force (internal or external) is not applied to mony, the money will continue to move at a constant velocity and zero acceleration.**

First, we define the acceleration of money. The acceleration of money is in fact the changes in the speed of money over time:

$$a_m = \frac{\partial V_m}{\partial t}$$

On the other hand, from the definition of the velocity of money, we will have:

$$V = \frac{r.MU_x}{B} \rightarrow \dot{V} = \dot{r} + M\dot{U}_x$$

Therefore, if the marginal utility of money substitutes is fixed ( $M\dot{U}_x = 0$ ) and also the interest rate remains unchanged ( $\dot{r} = 0$ ) then the velocity of money will remain constant ( $\partial V = 0$ ) so the acceleration of money will be zero (a = 0). Besides, from the quantity theory of money, we know that:

$$\dot{M} + \dot{V} = \dot{P} + \dot{Y}$$

Therefore, if P, Y and M do not change, the velocity of the money is constant ($\partial V = 0$), then the acceleration of money will be zero (a = 0)

In sum, two groups of internal and external forces will affect the velocity of money:

1. Internal forces: The marginal utility of money substitutes ($MU_x$) and interest rate (r)

2. External forces: Price (P), Production (Y) and Money Supply (M)

Changes in the first category certainly and directly affect the velocity of the money, but changes in the second category may or may not affect the velocity of the money.


**Law 2: Supposing that money supply is constant, economic growth is a factor in the acceleration of money.**

$G = k.a_m$

To prove the above equation, from the quantity theory of money, we have:

$P.Y = M.V$

Assuming that nominal production is P.Y, we will have:

$y = M.V$

Now, if we assume that for two consecutive years the money supply is constant, then we will take the derivative of both sides of the equation relative to time:

$$\frac{\partial y}{\partial t} = M.\frac{\partial V}{\partial t}$$

On the other hand, we have earlier called the changes in the velocity of money over time as acceleration of money:

$$\frac{\partial y}{\partial t} = M.a_m$$

Dividing both sides of the above equation by y, we will have:

$$\frac{\frac{\partial y}{\partial t}}{y} = \frac{M}{y}.a_m$$

On the one hand, the term ($\frac{M}{y}$) is the velocity of the money, or the coefficient (k) in the quantity theory of money. Also, the term in left-hand side that shows changes in production divided by production is the definition of economic growth. So we'll have it.

$$G = k.a_m$$

The coefficient k represents the average money supply per exchange. Therefore, it can be suggested in two consecutive years, if the money supply is constant, economic growth is a factor of acceleration of money.

**Law 3: In equilibrium, for every money supply, there is a money demand equal to it and in the opposite direction.**

Proof: In economic exchanges, each transaction is made up of a buyer and a seller, the buyer pays the money and at the same time the seller asks for the same money supply. Therefore, in exchange for any money supply, there is an equal demand in the opposite direction.

The three above laws are called laws of motion of money.

# Chapter 3

# How economic growth and business cycles come into existence?

Economists have always been attempting to figure out how the path of economic growth is determined and what the influential factors are. They, in particular, have been looking to persuasively explain the causes of difference among the economic growths of different countries. For this, a variety of economic growth models have been designed and proposed such as Harrod–Domar model, Solow Model, Ramsey economic growth model etc. However, all these model share the same major drawback. They all have studied a balanced path of long-term economic growths during courses of full employment and then have proposed a number of influential factors regarding this path. In fact, they all have considered equilibrium and full employment. However, they have failed to offer explanations for cases where the economy is in equilibrium, yet challenged by unemployment.

The real-world evidence shows that most countries face economic balance and unemployment at the same time, a phenomenon that has lasted over a long period of time. As a matter of fact, the long-term balanced growth path concurrently takes place with unemployment in most countries. We here attempt to give an account of the balanced economic growth path in presence of unemployment. We in fact intend to show how a country can access long-term balanced economic growth in spite of unemployment.

Economic growth models assume that the firms that produce commodities hire production agents from families and compensate them through the income of selling these commodities. Families in turn dedicate some of their income to consumption and save the balance. These savings are then given to firms for investment purposes. In other words, all the outputs of the economic cycle re-enter this cycle labeled as investments. However, this assumption is open to debate. Economic growth models often assume that the savings are either converted to investments by families through the mechanism of the market or a powerful government equals the savings and the investments.

We now want to slam this assumption. We in fact believe that not every saving is converted to investment, a factor that seems to be one of the causes of unemployment in the economic system.

Real-world observations show that families don't convert their whole savings into investments. Each family always keeps a share of their savings in form of money. It thus could be concluded that the money kept by families is in fact the saving that has left the cycle but will not return there. Therefore, a part of the savings (S) will not turn into investments (I). The question is this now: excluding the money, will the balances of the savings be converted to investments? Yes, we have two forms of investment: productive and unproductive.

Therefore, one can suggest that the savings of families will take three possible forms: they will either go to the productive investments (I), to the unproductive investments ($I'$) or kept as money (M). We thus come to:

$$S = I + I' + M$$

It is thus concluded that investments are not equal to savings and some part of the savings either take the form of money or unproductive investments. This leads us to:

$$S \neq I \rightarrow S > I$$

In other words, at the very least, some part of the savings are not converted to productive investments, the effects of which must be taken into account in economic growth models. Long-term economic growth plans must be designed to cover this issue.

First, let's present the whole saving as follows:

$$S = S_I + S_{I'} + S_M$$
$$S = I + I' + M$$
$$S = \phi S + \lambda S + \gamma S$$

So:

$$S = (\phi + \lambda + \gamma)S \rightarrow \phi + \lambda + \gamma = 1$$

In other words, the productive investment does not equal the whole savings or just a share of the savings is converted to productive investments:

$$I_t = \phi . S_{t-1}$$

On the other hand, we are aware that savings are a part of the income:

$$S_{t-1} = s.Y_{t-1}$$

We thus come to this:

$$I_t = \phi.s.Y_{t-1}$$

u is defined as the investment-to-production ratio:

$$u_t = \frac{K_t}{Y_t} \rightarrow K_t = u.Y_t$$

We also know that investment is the difference between the capitals of the current and former time periods:

$$I_t = K_t - K_{t-1}$$

Considering the investment-to-production ratio:

$$I_t = u.Y_t - u.Y_{t-1} = u.(Y_t - Y_{t-1})$$

Since we already have developed the investment function as below:

$$I_t = \phi.s.Y_{t-1}$$

We thus come to this after inserting the following relation in the above-mentioned equation:

$$\phi.s.Y_{t-1} = u.(Y_t - Y_{t-1})$$

We come to this after simplifying the relation:

$$\frac{Y_t - Y_{t-1}}{Y_{t-1}} = \frac{\phi.s}{u}$$

Economic growth is indicated on the left of the equation. Assuming that we are in the ideal state of Harrod–Domar model or when the saving ratio-to-investment ratio is equal to the population growth:

$$\frac{s}{u} = n$$

In other words, the conditions of "the golden age" are met. Even when these conditions are fulfilled, we have the following relation because $(0 < \phi < 1)$:

$$\frac{\phi.s}{u} < n$$

Thus this age is not as golden as it seems. In this state, economy faces demand shortages and there is unused capacity in the economy according to $(1-\phi)$. The unemployment rate will be in proportion to $(1-\phi)$ (Note that this unemployment exists even when the criterion of the golden age or $\frac{s}{u} = n$ is fulfilled.

If $\phi = 1$ (also when the golden age exists), economy will be in "full employment" status. However, if $\phi = 0$ and despite the existence of some savings $(S=s.Y)$, no part of these savings will be converted to productive investments and thus the whole economy does not produce anything which is the same as unemployment.

Let's take a different look at this argument:

$$\frac{\phi.s}{u} < n \rightarrow \frac{\phi.s}{K/Y} < n \rightarrow \phi.s.\frac{Y}{K} < n$$

$$\phi.s.\frac{Y/L}{K/L} < n \rightarrow \frac{\phi.s.y}{k} < n \rightarrow \phi.s.y < n.k$$

As a matter of fact, nk or the growth rate of the work force multiplied by the per capita capital of each member of the work force is the required capital for maintaining the per capita capital in the status quo and despite the population growth. On one hand, the quantity of $(\phi.s.y)$ is the same part of the savings which is converted to investments and on the other hand the per capita capital is defined as below:

$$k = \frac{K}{L} \rightarrow \frac{\dot{k}}{k} = \frac{\dot{K}}{K} - \frac{\dot{L}}{L}$$

On one hand the growth of the work force is $n = \frac{\dot{L}}{L}$ and on the other hand $(\dot{K} = I = \phi.s.Y)$. We thus come to the following after inserting these two in the above-mentioned equation:

$$\frac{\dot{k}}{k} = \frac{\phi.s.Y}{K} - n = \frac{\phi.s.Y/L}{K/L} - n \rightarrow \frac{\dot{k}}{k} = \frac{\phi.s.y}{k} - n$$

Simplifying the last phrase gives the following relation:

$$\Delta k = \phi.s.y - n.k$$

We have already learned that $(\phi.s.y < n.k)$ in the golden age and thus we get the following relation considering the above-mentioned relation:

$$\Delta k = \phi.s.y - n.k < 0$$

It means that the per capita capital decreases in spite of the occurrence of $\phi$ ($\Delta k<0$) which prompts decreases in both capital investment (k) and per capita production(y)(decreases in the per capita capital will take place at a faster rate than decreases in the per capita production) to restore new balance to the economy. Let's further the growth model via adopting Cobb-Douglas production function:

$$\Delta k = s.y - n.k$$

For starter, let's assume that $\phi=1$ or the whole saving is converted to investments (I=S=s.Y). We thus come to:

$$\Delta k = s.y - n.k$$

Sustainable balanced status is where:

$$\Delta k = 0 \rightarrow s.y = n.k$$

This equilibrium could be observed in the figure below, where Cobb-Douglass production function has been assigned a fixed efficiency in relation to the scale and the following conditions are at play:

$$Y = F(K,L) = K^{\alpha}.L^{1-\alpha}$$
$$f(\frac{K}{L}) = k^{\alpha} \rightarrow f'(k) \geq 0, f''(k) < 0$$

This figure shows the process of achieving the sustainable equilibrium point:

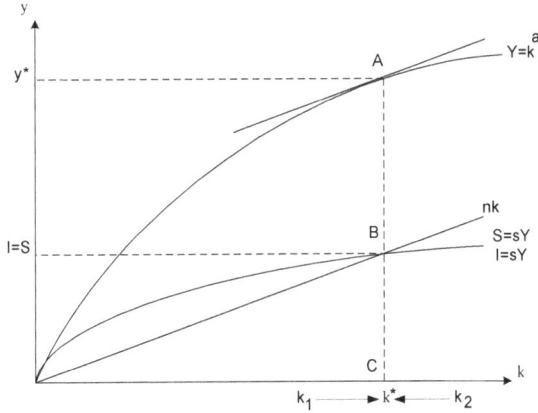

Figure 3.1: Optimal per capita capital from equality of savings and investment

$$y = k^{\alpha}$$

$$S = s.Y$$

This figure suggests that the per capita production follows the following production function:

$$y = k^{\alpha}$$

In addition, families save at rate s and thus the saving function is:

$$S = s.Y$$

The relation between investments at every moment and savings are:

$I = S = s.Y$

In fact, saving and investment functions are on two different slopes. However, they match on the figure because they are equal in this case.

Firms add these investments to their capital inventories. The per capita production is dependent on per capita capitals according to $y = k^\alpha$. The capital is accumulated based on the following relation:

$\Delta k = s.y - n.k$

In B we have:

$s.y = n.k$

Thus:

$\Delta k = 0$

This means that the per capita capital will not undergo changes. New capitals (sy) must equal the capital required for the new population (nk) if the per capita capital is going to remain unchanged. This has been illustrated in the figure above where a corporation of k capital produces y commodities which is the same as a family's income. Every individual saves a sum of BC and consumes AB. The whole of an individual's saving is converted into investments and thus the investments will be AB as it is the case for the savings.

This per capita capital $(k^*)$ is a sustainable balanced capital as s.y <n.k is seen on the right side of the point, similar to $k_2$. Thus, based on the

relation $\Delta k = s.y - n.k$, the per capita capital decreases to match $k^*$ where $s.y = nk$ and $\Delta k = 0$. On the left side of the point we have $s.y > n.k$ which means that the new investments surpass the volume required for the new population. As a result, the per capita capital increases to reach $k^*$.

It is of course clear that this point depends on the saving rate (s) and B moves in response to s variations. However, to make the assumptions simple, s has been selected according to Ramsey's growth model to maximize the per capita consumption, where $(f'(k) = n)$. This is an ideal state that produces the highest welfare. We can now acquire the optimal per capita capital $(k^*)$ as well as the optimal per capita income $(y^*)$. For this, we know that $\Delta k = 0$ is at point B and thus we have:

$$\Delta k = 0 \rightarrow s.y = n.k$$

On the other hand, Cobb-Douglass –type production function displays a constant return to scale:

$$k^* = (\frac{s}{n})^{\frac{1}{1-\alpha}}$$

$$y^* = (\frac{s}{n})^{\frac{\alpha}{1-\alpha}}$$

This is for cases where the whole saving is converted to the investment. However, we have already shown that:

$$S = \phi.S + \lambda.S + \gamma.S$$
$$S = I + I' + M$$

We also have this relation:

$$\phi + \lambda + \gamma = 1 \rightarrow \lambda + \gamma = 1 - \phi$$

And thus we could write:

$$S = \phi.S + (1-\phi).S \rightarrow S = I + (I' + M)$$

Therefore, a part of the saving will be converted into investments:

$$I = \phi.S$$

Now, the saving function does not equal the investment function and thus their curves do not match which is illustrated in the figure below:

$$\left.\begin{array}{l} S = s.Y \\ I = \phi.s.Y \end{array}\right\} \rightarrow I < S$$

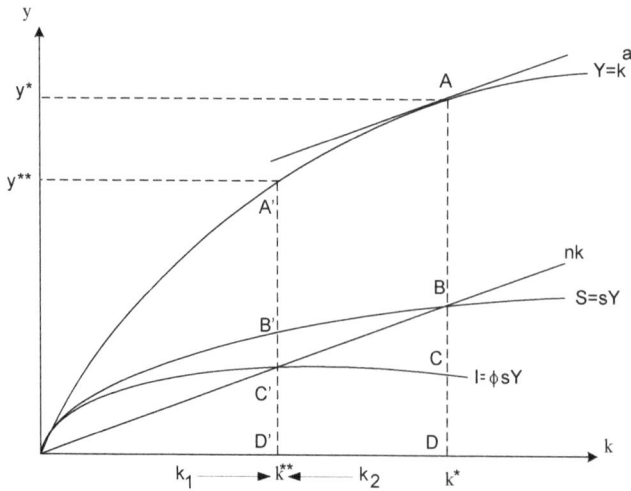

Figure 3.2: Optimal per capita capital when a part of savings turns into investment

According to this figure, in $k^*$ status, investments were lower than savings (S>I) and thus we got:

$$\Delta k = \phi.s.y - n.k$$

Since we observe the following relation in $k^*$:

$$\phi.s.y < n.k$$

As a result, $\Delta K < 0$ i.e. the per capita investments will decrease. This decrease prompts drops in the per capita capital (k) on one hand and increases the per capita income (y) on the other hand. In addition, since both the investments and the savings are dependent on the income:

$$S = s.Y$$
$$I = \phi.s.Y$$

Savings and investments thus decrease to bring the per capita investment to $k^{**}$. Here, A′D′ is produced and the individual saves a sum of B′D′ according to S=s.Y, a C′D′ of which is dedicated to productive investments based on I=$\phi$.S.Y and a B′C′ of which take the form of money or unproductive investments.

Now C′ is where $n.k = \phi.s.y$

$$\Delta k = \phi.s.y - n.k = 0$$

Thus this will be the new steady state, any departure from which will get us back to it. In other words, $\phi.s.y < n.k$ at point k2 and thus the per capita capital begins to decreases according to $\Delta k = \phi.s.y - n.k$ to reach $k^{**}$. On the other hand, $\phi.s.y > n.k$ is at k1 and thus the per capita capital begins to increases according to $\Delta k = \phi.s.y - n.k$ to reach $k^{**}$.

$k^{**}$ which is smaller than $k^{*}$ is the new steady state when savings and investments are not equal. It should be noted that this new point is both steady and balanced at the same time i.e. we have y long-term per capita income, $B'D'$ of which is saved and just a sum of $C'D'$ goes to investments while $B'C'$ of this income will be kept as money or is dedicated to unproductive investments which results in unemployment in proportion. In other words, this new point is both a balanced state and steady at the same time despite unemployment. We thus can contend that this pattern describes the steady, balanced long-term economic growth in spite of unemployment.

It should be noted that $(f'(k) \neq n)$. We will later show that the slope of production function at $A'$ is:

$$f'(k) = \frac{n}{\phi}$$

It means that the slope of this point is bigger than the slope of nk since $0 < \phi < 1$ and we have:

$$\frac{n}{\phi} > n$$

However, this point is both balanced and steady in spite of unemployment.

We could compute optimal per capita capital $(k^{**})$ and optimal per capita production $(y^{**})$ which gives us:

$$k^{**} = (\frac{\phi.s}{n})^{\frac{1}{1-\alpha}}$$

$$y^{**} = (\frac{\phi.s}{n})^{\frac{\alpha}{1-\alpha}}$$

We could see that $k^{**}$ is smaller than $k^{*}$ and $y^{**}$ is smaller than $y^{*}$ here which is also true for savings, investments and consumption. This all could be associated with $(I'+M)$ i.e. the larger the shares of money and unproductive investments or when $(1-\phi)$ is bigger and $(\phi)$ is smaller, the slope of $(\phi.s.y)$ moves down to intersect n.k slop at a lower point which cuts the per capita investments and production. Increased $(\phi)$ will prompt dedication of more shares into productive investments which in turn raises the per capita investments and production, leading to the achievement of an ideal status or $(\phi = 1)$. In other words, the unemployment will be in proportion to $(I'+M)$ which is computed as below:

$$\frac{I'+M}{I+I'+M} = \frac{B'C'}{A'D'} = \frac{s.y-\phi.s.y}{s.y} = \frac{(1-\phi).s.y}{s.y} = (1-\phi)$$

If $\phi = 0$, the whole saving will be idle while $\phi = 1$ means no idle savings exists and the capital is fully employed:

So far we have focused on the acquisition of optimal per capita capitals and optimal per capita incomes. The closer the $\phi$ to one, the shorter the gap between per capita capitals and production and their ideal state while smaller $\phi$ (when $1-\phi$ is bigger) pushes the per capita capitals and production away from their ideal state.

We will attempt to study the effects of the inequality between the investment and savings on the consumption and welfare of the society. Let's imagine that families choose to accumulate capitals through savings and lay the grounds for the growth in future periods on one hand and maximize their welfare via choosing consumption on the other hand. The question now is choosing the optimal option between savings and consumption to maximize the life time welfare of an individual. The individual's utility function is:

$$U = \int u(c(t)).e^{-\rho}dt$$

Where $\rho$ is the time preference rate and will grow larger should the individual assign less value to their future consumption compared to their current rate of consumption. The utility function is as below:

$$u(c(t)) = \frac{c(t)^{1-\theta}}{1-\theta}$$

The above-mentioned function is called Constant Relative Risk Aversion (CRRA) utility function where the risk aversion coefficient or $\theta$ of this function is computed as below:

$$\theta = \frac{-c.u''(c(t))}{u'(c(t))}$$

Where, the phrase $\sigma = \dfrac{1}{\theta}$ is the substitution elasticity between consumption at two time points. Utility maximization is the goal or U maximization which has already been introduced. However, constraints on capital accumulation are the issue. Capital accumulation model is as follows:

$$k = \frac{K}{L} \rightarrow \frac{\dot{k}}{k} = \frac{\dot{K}}{K} - \frac{\dot{L}}{L} \rightarrow \frac{\dot{k}}{k} = \frac{I}{K} - n \rightarrow \frac{\dot{k}}{k} = \frac{\phi.S}{K} - n$$

We already know that the saving is the surplus of income after deducting the consumption:

$$\frac{\dot{k}}{k} = \frac{\phi.(Y-C)}{K} - n \rightarrow \frac{\dot{k}}{k} = \frac{\phi.Y/L}{K/L} - \frac{\phi.C/L}{K/L} - n \rightarrow \dot{k} = \phi.y - \phi.c - n.k$$

We thus have to deal with the goal function and the following constraint:

$$\text{MAX}: U = \int u(c(t)).e^{-\rho} dt$$

$$\dot{k} = \phi.f(k) - \phi.c - n.k$$

We could write a Hamilton function for resolving the above-mentioned question:

$$H = u(c(t)) + \mu \left[ \phi.f(k) - \phi.c - n.k \right]$$

The first-degree condition could be written as below if we intend to find the optimal paths for variables:

$$\frac{\partial H}{\partial c} = u'(c) - \mu = 0 \rightarrow u'(c) = \mu$$

$$\dot{\mu} = -\mu.\phi.f'(k) + n.\mu + \rho.\mu$$

$$\dot{k} = \phi.f(k) - \phi.c - n.k$$

If we develop a derivative from ($u'(c) = \mu$) relation relative to the time:

$$\frac{\partial(u'(c))}{\partial t} = \dot{\mu}$$

If we substitute this relation in the above-mentioned equation:

$$u''(c)\frac{dc}{dt} = \dot{\mu} = -\mu.\phi.f'(k) + (n+\rho).\mu$$

$$u''(c).\dot{c}(t) = -\mu[\phi.f'(k) - (n+\rho)]$$

So we could write this:

$$\frac{-u''(c)}{u'(c)}\dot{c}(t) = \frac{\theta(c)}{c(t)}\dot{c}(t) = \phi.f'(k) - (n+\rho)$$

We thus could extract the relation below from the combination of important relations regarding the paths of per capita consumption growth and per capita capital accumulation:

$$\dot{c}(t) = \frac{1}{\theta(c)}[\phi.f'(k) - (n+\rho)].c(t)$$

$$\dot{k} = \phi.f(k) - \phi.c - n.k$$

These paths have been displayed in the space (c,k) in this figure:

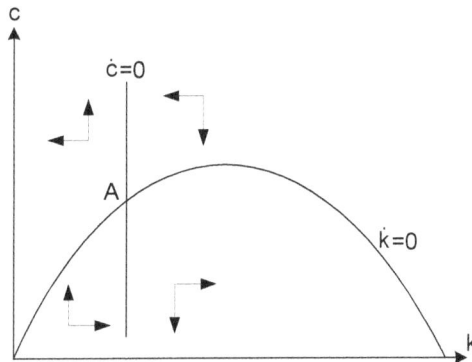

Figure 3.3: Equilibrium between per capita consumption and per capita capital

Consumption should be $\dot{c} = 0$ if achieving the optimal consumption point is intended:

$$\dot{c} = 0 \rightarrow \phi.f'(k) = n + \rho$$

$\dot{c} = 0$ line has been marked in this figure. As the figure suggests, if k is smaller than $k_0$, f'(k) has increased and so $\phi.f'(k) > n + \rho$. Therefore, $\dot{c} > 0$ which means that per capita consumption (c) is on the rise. If k is found to be bigger than $k_0$, f'(k) will decrease and thus $\phi.f'(k) < n + \rho$ and $\dot{c} > 0$ i.e. the per capita consumption is on the rise. As a result, the consumption will have a zero growth on so $\phi.f'(k) = n + \rho$ line. This could be written as follows:

$$f'(k) = \frac{n+\rho}{\phi}$$

$\dot{k} = 0$ must be established if achieving the optimal capital accumulation point is intended:

$$\dot{k} = 0 \rightarrow \phi[f(k) - c(t)] = n.k$$

As the figure suggests, the per capita consumption has increased over $\dot{k} = 0$ and $\phi[f(k) - c(t)] < n.k$ and thus $\dot{k} < 0$ and capital accumulation (k) will start to decrease. In addition, if the per capita consumption (c) decreases under $\dot{k} = 0$ and $\phi[f(k) - c(t)] > n.k$ · As a result, $\dot{k} < 0$ and capital accumulation (k) will start to decrease. This condition $\dot{k} = 0$ could be rewritten as follows:

$$f(k) - c(t) = \frac{n}{\phi}k$$

Considering the previous fuzzy model, the A point is the steady state on the saddle-horse graph where $K_0$ and $c_0$ represent capital accumulation and balance consumption, respectively. $T_0$ concentrate on the effects of the changes in $\phi$, we assume that the time preference rate of the society is at the optimal state or zero and thus the steady state is achieved as result of the meeting of two lines of $\dot{k} = 0$ and $\dot{c} = 0$. Therefore, A will be the steady state. The figure below has been drawn assuming a zero time preference rate:

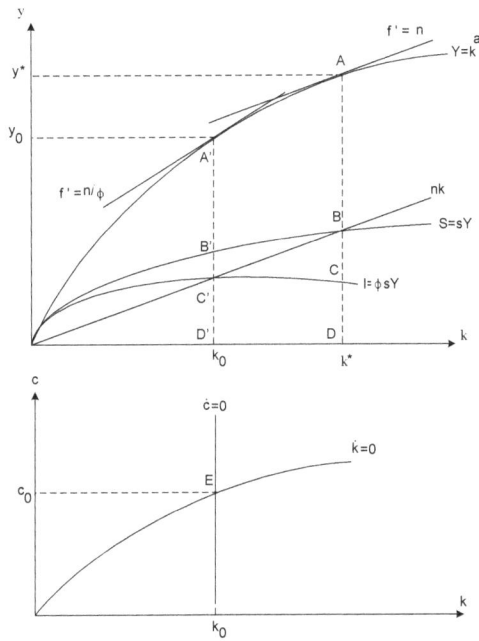

Figure 3.4: Per capita consumption when a part of savings turns into investment

This is the steady state so the per capita production will be $y_0$ in each time period, where $c_0$ is the per capita consumption and $s_0 = y_0 - c_0$ is the share that is dedicated to per capita savings. Part of this saving ( $I_0 = \phi.s_0$ ) is spent on productive investments while another share ( $I' + M = (1-\phi)S_0$ ) goes to unproductive investments or kept as money.

As it is obvious, despite the fact that the time preference rate is zero ($\rho=0$), the society is yet to achieve its maximum per capita consumption, capital and production and thus $(1-\phi)$ of the capital stays idle and the economy faces steady unemployment.

It should be noted that the unemployment is at a steady state and there is no force to move away from this point to reach the optimal point. As the time preference rate is zero ($\rho=0$), we come to the following relation considering the relation:

$$f'(k) = \frac{n}{\phi}$$

Since $(0 < \phi < 1)$, then $f'(k) > n$. Now, if a bigger part of the society dedicates its share of savings to the productive investments which decreases the shares of unproductive investments and money, we have the following relation according to $\dot{c} = 0$:

$$(\rho = 0) \rightarrow \phi.f'(k) = n$$

Increased $\phi$ will push $\dot{c} = 0$ curve to the right. Moreover, this increase moves $\dot{k} = 0$ curve upside.

Thus, when $\phi = 1$ or when the whole savings goes to productive investments and no share is assigned to unproductive investments or kept as money, the economy will move from E to F.

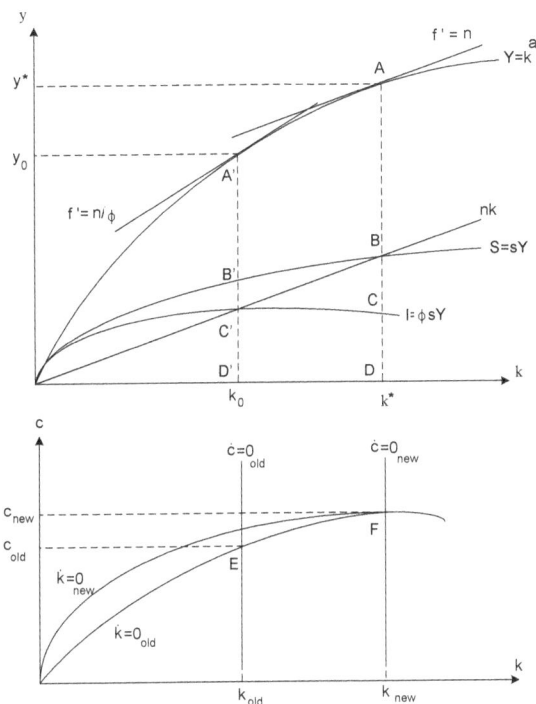

Figure 3.5: Per capita consumption when the entire savings turn into investment

As the graph suggests, increased $\phi$ and the economy's movement from $C'$ towards B point prompts the per capita investments to approach per capita savings. The whole saving goes to the productive investments at B point and consequently the per capita production increases. Also, according to the figure below, moving to F from E prompts increases in both per capita consumption and capitals.

The slope of the per capita production curve is:

$$f'(k) = \frac{n}{\phi}$$

The slope of the per capita production curve will be blunter as a result of increases in $\phi$ and if $\phi = 1$, then $f'(k) = n$. Since $f'(k)$ represents

The marginal efficiency of capital, increases in $\phi$ encourage higher employment rates of the capitals and consequently The marginal efficiency of capital decrease to reach $n$ value. It generally could be concluded that a part of capital equal to $(1-\phi)$ will always remain idle. The bigger the $\phi$, the higher the increases in the productive investments and the consumption and thus the society will have much better welfare. Maximum welfare will be reached at $\phi = 1$. This steady, new balance is at the time of full employment.

As already stated, the bigger the $\phi$ or the share of the productive part from the whole savings $\dfrac{I}{I + I' + M} = \dfrac{I}{S} = \phi$, a larger economic capacity is utilized while the bigger the shares of the unproductive investments $((1-\phi).S)$ or the money $((\lambda + \gamma).S)$, the larger the unused capacity of the economy i.e. the unemployment will be in proportion to $((\lambda + \gamma).S$ ) or the unused capacity of the economy $((1-\phi).S)$. This indicates that the economy has not utilized all of its available capitals and as a result a part of this capital has not been dedicated to $((1-\phi).S)$ in proportion to which (idle capitals) we have unemployed work force. The existence of idle capitals and unemployed work force means that the economy has failed to produce on the production possibility curve. Instead, it is inside this curve on a point similar to E which means a part of the economic resources is not utilized. The economy, consequently, fails to utilize its full capacity and thus slips into incomplete unemployed.

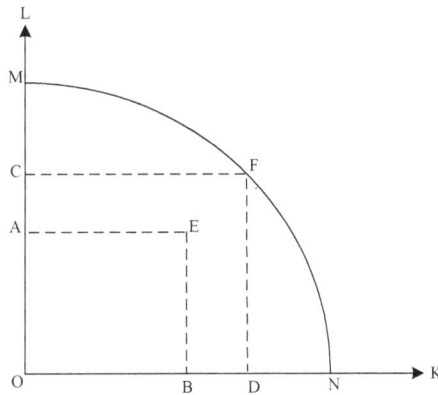

Figure 3.6: The production possibility curve

The ideal condition (F) is where ($\phi = 1$) i.e. the whole savings are spent on productive investments ($S = I$) while the savings which either go to unproductive investments or kept as money are minimized ($I' + M = 0$). When ($\phi = 1$), the country manages to utilize all its available resources and the economy is in full operation capacity i.e. the production is on its proper curve and the production resources are not idle (whether capitals or work force) which places employment in full employment status.

**- Business cycle models**

As already demonstrated, the savings are divided in three categories: a part ($\phi.S$) goes to productive investments (I), the second part ($\lambda.S$)

goes to productive investments ($I'$) and the last part ($\gamma.S$) is kept as money (M).

As the models of economic growth show, economic production and growth depends on the share of productive investments from the total savings ($\phi.S$). On the other hand, we have unused economic capacity in proportion to the total of unproductive investments and money ( $(1-\phi).S$) which define the rate of unemployment.

We have already stated that $\phi$ is defined between 0 and 1. The closer it is to 1, the closer the economy is to full employment while closer it gets to zero, the economy faces more intense recession and unemployment. This demonstrates the essential role played by $\phi$ in creation of recession and booms which justifies the importance of identifying this parameter and how it affects the economy. We here attempt to show that $\phi$ value is not randomly decided but is constantly fluctuating between 0 and zero because of the nature of the economy. This fluctuation brings constant and intermittent recession and boom periods which creates business cycles.

To create and study business cycle models, we first analyze the developments of the productive and unproductive and money.

**- The Productive Sector**

The amount of productive investments is indicated by I while the efficiency of each unit of productive investment is represented by r. Therefore, the total output of the productive investments ($TR_I$) is:

$$TR_I = r.I$$

On the other hand, since this output is uncertain and probable and considering the randomness of r, the income of the productive investment ($TR_I$) is random. Applying the rules of statistics, we use the standard deviation as an indicator of dispersion and the risk associated with the Efficiency of Investment. The risk of the income associated with productive investments ($\sigma_{TR_I}$) is equal to the risk of each investment unit multiplied by the total productive investment:

$$\sigma_{TR_I} = \sigma_r.I$$

Since the standard deviation is greater than bigger dispersion and variance and thus could be used an indicator of risk.

The previous equation gives us:

$$I = \frac{\sigma_{TR_I}}{\sigma_r}$$

If we insert this in the first equation:

$$TR_I = \frac{r.\sigma_{TR_I}}{\sigma_r}$$

We have found out two essential relations so far:

The first relation or $I = \dfrac{\sigma_{TR_I}}{\sigma_r}$ indicates that larger investments expose the resulting income to higher risks and dispersion. This relation has been demonstrated in the space$(I, \sigma_{TR_I})$on the right side coordinates and displays how the productive investments and the risk of income associated with this type of investments are directly related.

The second relation or $TR_I = \dfrac{r.\sigma_{TR_I}}{\sigma_r}$ indicates that higher income requires having to take more risks. This relation has been demonstrated on the space $TR_I, \sigma_{TR_I}$ on the left side coordinates and shows the direct relation between the productive investments and the risk of income associated

with this type of investments.

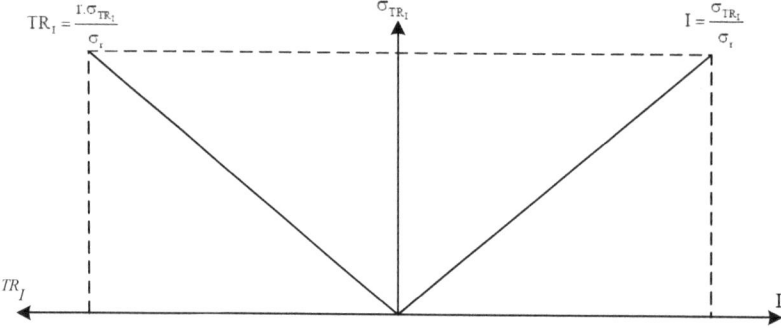

Figure 3.7: Maximum productive investment

As the figure suggests, the maximum available productive investment is equal to the whole savings where the risks taken are at their highest levels and naturally the highest anticipated income is obtained.

On the other hand, productive investments ( $TR_I$ ) enhance an individual's utility while the risk associated with the income of such investments ($\sigma_{TR_I}$) decrease the individual's utility. Therefore, in case of $TR_I, \sigma_{TR_I}$ where the risk increases, the utility of an individual depends on achieving higher anticipated incomes. The even utility function for a risk-evading individual could be drawn in $TR_I, \sigma_{TR_I}$ space:

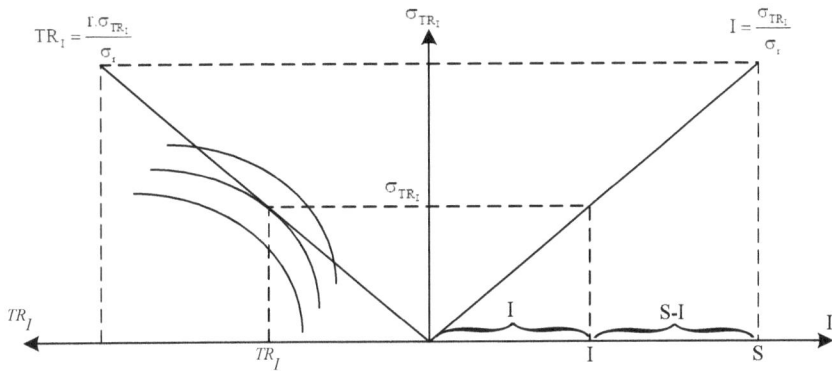

Figure 3.8: Selecting the optimal productive investment volume

The optimal point is where $TR_I = \dfrac{r.\sigma_{TR_I}}{\sigma_r}$ meets the highest utility function, for obtaining of which (or the highest income or $TR_I^{*}$) one has to take risks ($\sigma^{*}_{TR_I}$). This level of risk is a result of investing I* for productive purposes. Therefore, the amount of I* from the whole S or in other words $\phi$ percent of the whole savings will go to productive investments.

## - The Unproductive Sector

The amount of unproductive investments is indicated by $I'$ while the efficiency of each unit of productive investment is represented by i. Therefore, the total return of the productive investments ($TR_{I'}$) is:

$$TR_{I'} = i.I'$$

On the other hand, since return of every unproductive sector is a random variable, we again use the standard deviation for revealing the risks associated with unproductive investments. Therefore, the total risks associated with unproductive investments $\sigma_{TR_{I'}}$ are equal the risks associated with each unit of unproductive investment $\sigma_i$ multiplied by the volume of unproductive investment:

$$\sigma_{TR_{I'}} = \sigma_i.I'$$

We thus could come to this:

$$I' = \frac{\sigma_{TR_{I'}}}{\sigma_i}$$

If we insert this in the previous equation:

$$TR_{I'} = i.\frac{\sigma_{TR_{I'}}}{\sigma_i}$$

We have found out two essential relations so far:

The first relation or $I' = \dfrac{\sigma_{TR_{I'}}}{\sigma_i}$ indicates that increased unproductive investments lead to more risks. As the coordinates on the left side show, $I'$ and $\sigma_{TR_{I'}}$ are directly related.

The second relation or $TR_{I'} = i.\dfrac{\sigma_{TR_{I'}}}{\sigma_i}$ indicates that securing higher expected incomes in this sector entails taking more risks. As the coordinates on the left side show, $TR_{I'}$ and $\sigma_{TR_{I'}}$ are directly related.

Also, the equal utility functions are developed in $\sigma_{TR_{I'}}, TR_{I'}$ for a risk-averse individual in the unproductive investment sector.

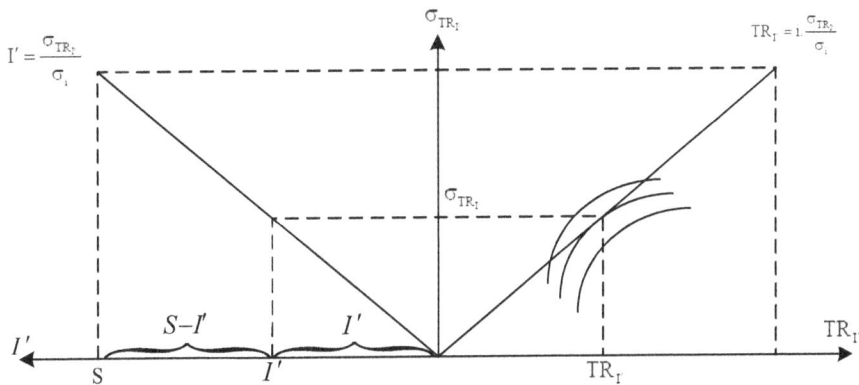

Figure 3.9: Selecting the optimal nonproductive investment volume

The above figure shows the contact point of $TR_{I'} = i.\dfrac{\sigma_{TR_{I'}}}{\sigma_i}$ and the highest utility function of the optimal point. It also specifies the unproductive investments and thus an $I'$ value of the whole savings goes to unproductive investments.

## - The kept money sector:

As already stated, once the savings are either allocated to productive or unproductive investments, The remaining part is kept as money (M). The following figure could be drawn through the combination of the figures for the unproductive and productive figures:

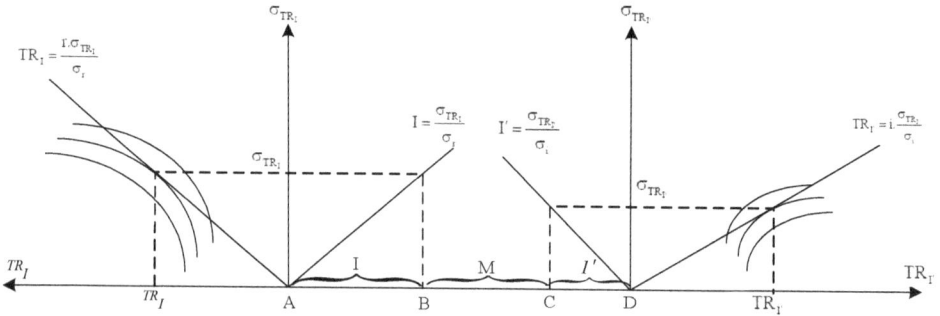

Figure 3.10: The optimal the kept money supply

As the figure shows, the whole savings are represented by the middle section while the left and the right sides represent productive and unproductive investments, respectively. The remaining part thus shows the kept money:

The share of the productive investments from the whole savings is:

$$\frac{I}{S} = \frac{AB}{AD} = \phi$$

The share of the unproductive investments from the whole savings is:

$$\frac{I'}{S} = \frac{CD}{AD} = \lambda$$

The share of the money kept from the whole savings is:

$$\frac{M}{S} = \frac{BC}{AD} = \gamma$$

After considering the developments in those three parts (productive sector, unproductive sector and the kept money sector).We now turn to introducing business cycle patterns:

Every economy goes through these stages on a regular basis:

1.  The whole saving is divided into productive investments, unproductive investments and the kept money where the marginal utility of the marginal return of all three components are equal.

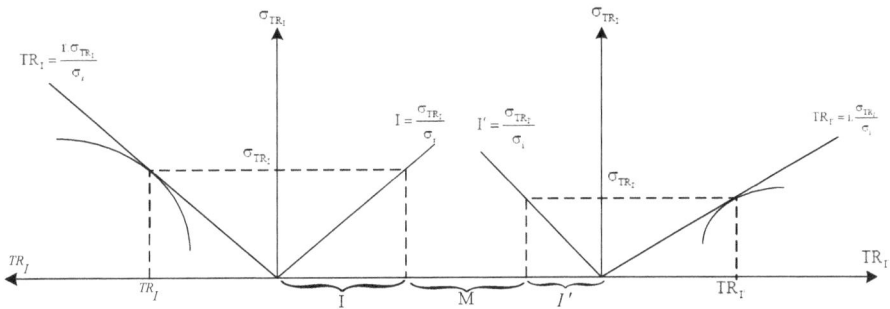

Figure 3.11: Productive and nonproductive investments and optimal the kept money supply

2.  As investments grow in the productive sector and over the time, the return of this sector decreases according to the principle of "diminishing marginal return". The productive investments decrease (the saving dedicated to this sector) as a result of drops in the productivity of the productive investments in comparison to other sectors.

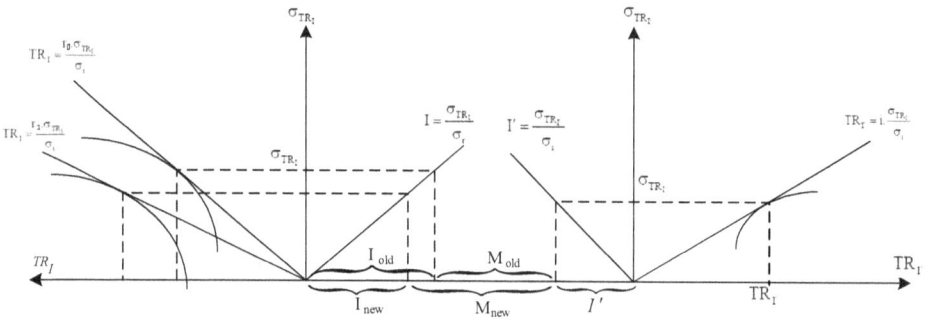

Figure 3.12: The effect of increasing the productive sector's return on equilibrium

3. Decreased return of productive sector results into lower dedication of the savings and as a result, the kept money increases. However, increases in money lower its marginal utility and thus a part of the savings goes to unproductive sector. Now, the return of the productive sector equals the marginal utility of the money. However, the marginal utility of the unproductive sector is still higher and attracts the savings. Increases in unproductive investments improve its return and thus could draw more savings.

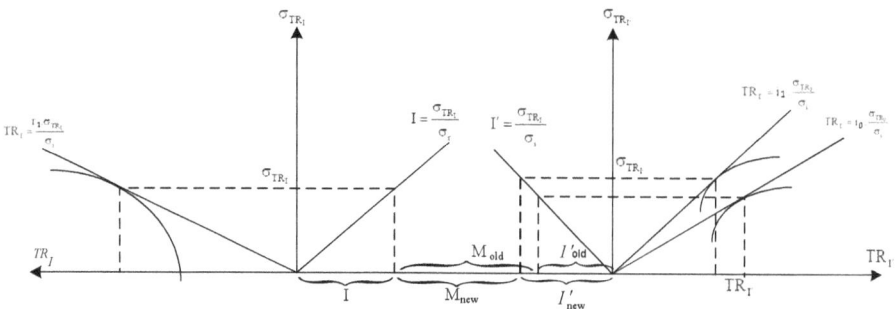

Figure 3.13: The effect of increasing the nonproductive sector's return on equilibrium

4. Since increased investments in the unproductive sector improve the return, a big bubble starts to develop which will burst as a result of the spread of a "psychological prompter" such as a gossip. Consequently, the risk spreads to unproductive sector and then to the productive sector which reduces the shares of these sectors from the savings. As a result, larger shares of the money are kept and the economy is embroiled in a liquidity trap (therefore liquidity traps will definitely develop after bursts of bubbles).

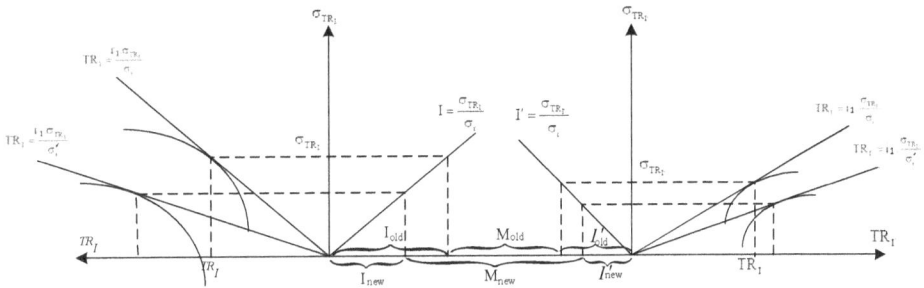

Figure 3.14: The effect of decreasing the productive and unproductive sectors' return on equilibrium

5. On one hand, when the "psychological prompter" loses its momentum the risks present in the economy are reduces and on the other hand, the return of the productive sector improves as a result of lowered productive investments. As a result of lowered risks and improved return of the productive sector, the investments in this sector tends to rise to a point where the return decreases according to the principle of "diminishing marginal return" and equals the return of two other sectors. This returns the economy to its first stage.

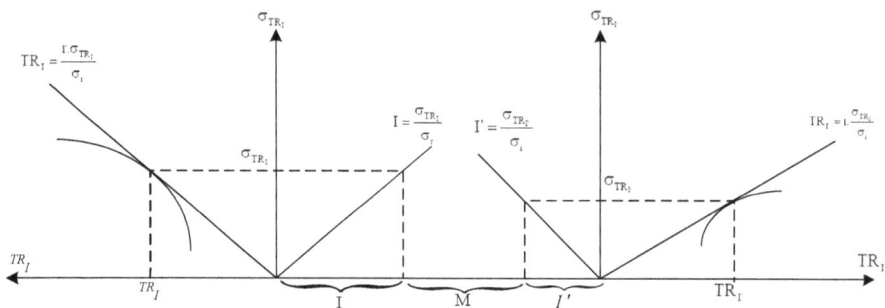

Figure 3.15: The equality of productive and nonproductive sectors'
returns and the kept money in equilibrium

As already stated, the whole savings (S) are divided into productive (
$I = \phi.S$ ), unproductive ( $I' = \lambda.S$ ) and money ( $M = \gamma.S$ ) while the
production depends on the share of productive investments ( $\phi$ ). We
have already stated that $\phi$ is defined between 0 and 1. The closer it is
to 1, the closer the economy is to full employment while the closer it
gets to zero; the economy faces more intense recession and
unemployment. In other words, $1-\phi$ indicates the untapped capacity
of the economy in proportion to which unemployment exists.

Economy starts from the stage one and reaches the fifth stage after
passing through the above-mentioned stages. This cycle is repeated on
a regular basis. The share which is dedicated to the productive sector (
$\phi$ ) varies in each stage and thus the used capacity of the economy
changes intermittently. Moreover, the unused capacity of the
economy changes intermittently and thus the economy and the
production and consequently the employment go through intermittent,
variable cycles. Therefore, the economy experience intermittent

cycles and boom and recession. As it was stated earlier about economic growth models, if S =1, that is $\phi = 1$, the per capita income will at last become convergent in the following amount:

$$y^* = (\frac{S}{n})^{\frac{1}{1-\alpha}}$$

This value is the long-term per capita income shown on the left side of the figure.

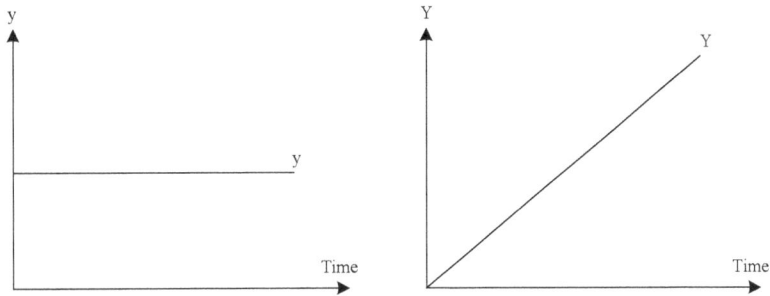

Figure 3.16: Total income and per capita income

On the other hand, we know that $y = \frac{Y}{N}$ and thus for Y to converge with its long-term value, its growth rate must be similar to the increases in the population. The population growth has been drawn on the right side of the figure. However, as already indicated, $0 < \phi < 1$ which means that a part of the savings go to productive investments ( $I = \phi.S$ ) which leads us to:

$$y^* = (\frac{\phi.S}{n})^{\frac{1}{1-\alpha}}$$

We have shown in business cycle models that $\phi$ is constantly fluctuating between zero and one. Therefore, the per capita income constantly approaches and moves away from its long-term projections which have been displayed on the left figure. Also, the total income which has been displayed on the right figure in proportion to per capita incomes constantly approaches and moves away from its potential value.

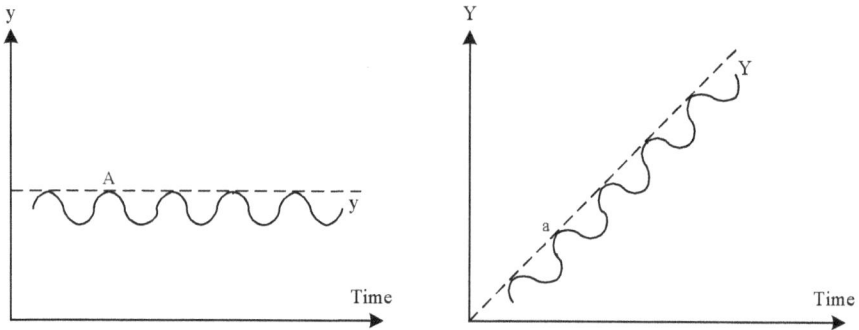

Figure 3.17: Business cycles in total and per capita income

For example $\phi$ in the A point in the left figure is equal to 1 ($\phi=1$) and thus the per capita production and the total production could achieve their potential values:

$$y^* = (\frac{\phi.s}{n})^{\frac{1}{1-\alpha}} \rightarrow if(\phi = 1) \rightarrow y^* = (\frac{s}{n})^{\frac{1}{1-\alpha}}$$

This phrase is essentially composed of two parts:

$$y^* = (\phi)^{\frac{1}{1-\alpha}} (\frac{s}{n})^{\frac{1}{1-\alpha}}$$

The first part shows the short path of business cycles while the second part shows the long-term path of economic growth.

As already demonstrated by business cycle models, $\phi$ is constantly fluctuating between zero and one and thus the economy constantly approaches or moves away of its potential values (the long-term growth) which bring about these cycles and therefore the first part $(\phi)^{\frac{1}{1-\alpha}}$ displays the short path of business cycles. However, as previously shown, the optimal long-term income converges at $(\frac{s}{n})^{\frac{1}{1-\alpha}}$ value and thus the second part shows the long-term economic growth.

In the next chapter, we will discuss the policies that guide $\phi$ value to one specific direction and realize the potential production to remove business cycles. We will also propose policies for reaching the optimal points.

# Chapter 4

# What should be done?

We first explored the function of economy in the first chapter. For this, we started from the simplest operation in the economy (transactions) and found out that the world of economy is composed of values transferred among individuals. These values are converted into new values through labor to satisfy a utility. We found out at the end of that chapter that in transactions of barter economies, value supplies and demands are always equal and take place at the same time. However, this type of economy has been replaced with monetary economy where money mediates the transactions and is in fact a channel in which values flow. We have observed that half of the transaction or supply of the value and demand for the money takes place yet its second part or money supplies and value demands fail to be completed, the result of which is shortages of value demands equal to the available idle money. We also concluded that money found utility over time and moved away from its original mission (flow the values), i.e. money became a goal itself. Money utility was discussed in the second chapter.

We addressed the functions of the money in economy in the second chapter. For this, money utility was the first topic discussed. It was demonstrated that the availability of money comforted the individual and thus money had utility per se. Having included the money in the utility function, we concluded that balance took place at a point where the relative marginal utility of the money equaled the relative marginal utility of its substitutes. Drawing on the quantity theory of the money, we showed that the optimal volume of money growth had to equal the sum of productivity and population growth rates if we intended to achieve fixed money marginal utility as well as fixed prices. We also demonstrated the factors influencing the money velocity. This is an important point as we know that economic growth is a coefficient of money acceleration in case the money volume is fixed. How money affects the economic growth was addressed in the third chapter.

Discussing economic growth models was the starting point of the third chapter. We first criticized the notion of the equality of savings and investments and demonstrated that only a share of savings would be converted to productive investments while the balance would either go to unproductive investments or take the form of idle money. Having corrected these assumptions in Harod-Domar, Solow and Ramsey models, we proceeded to show that the production decreased in proportion to the shares of the savings which were dedicated to unproductive investments or kept as idle money, resulting into unemployment and drops of per capita production, income and even per capita consumption. This hinders the economy from reaching the available ideal landmark. We in fact showed, via adopting economic growth models, that the part of the potential production which was realized was in proportion to the percentage of savings which was dedicated to productive investments. This was represented by $\phi$. Then through developing a business cycle model we managed to show that the economy constantly went through an intermittent round of stages through which $\phi$ was fluctuating between zero and one. As a result, the economic growth and per capita production approached and moved away from their potential value, thus giving rise to business cycles.

The whole discussion up to this point could be summarized as follows:

The whole economic welfare is composed of utilities which are satisfied by the created values. Values are converted into newer values by labor while the money is a channel for moving these values. However, the problem came up when the money found utility itself which leads to the idleness of a part of it in proportion to which the production is pushed away from its potential value. The money velocity and acceleration must be maximized if the ideal point and the maximum of potential production are intended. This requires that the money marginal utility is minimized.

We attempt in this chapter to answer this question: what should be done and what policies must be adopted to achieve this objective?

We first have to learn the influences of any given policy before answering this question: any proposed policy should seek to maximize the money velocity and acceleration if it intends to eliminate money utility. In other words, it must remove the saving incentive of the money and minimize the idle money.

It is proposed to impose tax on money to reduce its saving incentive, maximize the money velocity and achieve optimal economic status. As a matter o fact and as demonstrated before, the economy faces demand shortages equal to the available idle money in proportion to which recession and unemployment come into existence. Common policies to redress the outcomes of idle money could be placed into two categories: monetary policies that suggest publication of new money to the extent of the available idle money and financial policies that suggest that government must create budget deficit equal to the savings which have left the economic cycle in form of idle money. Although seem suitable at the first look, they both bring about detrimental outcomes, the most important of which is distancing the economy from the automatic mechanism of the free market. In fact, these policies don't get into the core of the problem.

Regarding monetary policy, it is important to note two points: Firstly, how is it possible to ensure that the new printed money will not fall into the fate of the previous money and not become a treasure? Secondly, how one can guarantee that by the introduction of new money, the previous money does not come into circulations and make the money supply out of control. Therefore, in both cases, the money supply (the stock of money in circulation and velocity of money) will be getting out of the control of monetary authorities, but by imposing a tax policy on money, since all available money flows at the maximum velocity, and the stock of money will be fixed and under the control of monetary authorities.

Two important points should be mentioned about financial policy: Firstly, the government is not a good spender compared to people and the market mechanism. The second point is that the government will meet any increase in its expenditure by imposing taxes and, as it was stated earlier; taxes instead of being levied on people hindering production are imposed on those who are more productive.

The problem essentially is that a part of the savings has left the economic cycle in form of idle money. The correct suggestion would be delivering a force to the system in order to encourage individuals re-inject the idle money into the economy. For this, imposing tax on money is suggested to force the idle money back into the economy. Tax-on-money policy has a clear advantage over the afore-mentioned policies: the individual decides through the market system how to re-introduce the idle money to the cycle. In fact, the tax policy forces the individual find the best and most effective solution to re-introduce their money (considering the market mechanism).

There are a total of five reasons why tax should be imposed on money:

**The first reason:** Every commodity in the economy finally goes old, rusty, out of fashion, thus depreciating over time. However, it is only the money that has idiosyncratic advantages over any other commodity in which it neither goes rusty, old and out of fashion, nor does it depreciate it value and the fact that it will always keeps its value. These characteristics give the money the winning edge over any other asset and thus the owner of the money (demander of the commodities) has an apparent advantage over other commodity holders (suppliers of the commodities). This is true for every commodity and generally for the commodity market. Money holders may postpone their commodity demands to the future while commodity holders face the risk of commodity depreciation and storage costs due to postponements of demands. Money is the victor in this unfair contest.

This advantage reigns over the labor market as well. The employer (holder of the money) is confident that money will keep its value while the laborer (labor holder) feels pressure to offer their labor as the labor force will depreciate over time and thus has to make some expenses (accommodation, clothing, food etc) to preserve the status quo. Again, money will emerge victor in this unfair contest.

Therefore, money holders enjoy advantages which make competitions unfair in both commodity and labor markets. To establish a fair competition, the asset of the money holder should depreciate over time like the holders of commodities and labor. The depreciation rate could be established via imposing tax on money.

**The second reason:** The longer the money goes idle, the more resources are left to rot as a result of which the unemployment intensifies. Therefore, the longer the duration of money idleness, the more transfer of current values and creation of new values are suspended. Shorter "money stoppage time" is thus suggested to re-ignite value flows. "The money stoppage time period" could be computed through the following relation:

$$TM = \frac{T}{V+1}$$

Where TM is the time the money is stopped, T is the time period and V is the velocity of money. Should we consider the time period as one year or 365 days:

$$TM = \frac{365}{V+1}$$

If the velocity of money is zero, the TM will be 365 days. In other words, every monetary unit has on average been stopped or been idle for 365 days. If the velocity of money is four, it means that every monetary unit has on average been exchanged four times and thus the TM will be 73 days according to the relation above. In other words, each monetary unit has been idle after each round of exchange (of the total four).

Now we have learned about "the money stoppage time", we seek to know what forces move the money and shorten this stoppage time. We have already come to know external and internal forces influencing the velocity of money. Interest rate (r) and general prices (P) play crucial roles in this process.

As a matter of fact, the money holder feels the pressure of the punishment lever and the reward lever at the same time. The punishment lever is the general level of prices; increases in prices bring down purchase power which punishes money holders in the end and push them to start re-introducing their money into economy while the reward lever is the interest rate which encourages the money holders to relinquish money idling in order to enjoy the interest rate.

Therefore, increases in both Interest rate (r) and general prices (ρ) exert pressure on the money in order to enhance its velocity and shorten the "money stoppage time". However, it should be noted that simultaneous increases in both prices and the interest rate leave detrimental impacts on the economy. Therefore, another must should be planned to prompt money flows and shorten the "money stoppage time". This force could be delivered through imposing tax on money with the added value that it does not bring about the detrimental impacts of increases in both prices and the interest rate.

**The Third Reason:** We learned that value supplies and demands take place at the same time in barter economies. In other words, the individual demands value (demands for commodities) at the same time they supply it (supply of commodities). However, when money is available, value supplies and demands take place at two separate money-mediated transactions. It means that an individual supplies values in a transaction, receives money in exchange and then supplies money in another transaction to demand value.

In fact, money is channel through which economic values could start to flow and thus it must play a mediating role for value supplies and demands. However, as already suggested, money found utility through storage of values. To counteract this utility, some forms of tax must be imposed on the money so the money could revert to its original mediating, connecting role. Therefore, imposition of some tax on money is suggested.

**The Fourth Reason:** Individuals are placed in two categories based on how they use their savings: 1. those who convert their savings into investments, 2. those who don't flow their savings. The current taxing system taxes the first group but leaves the second group alone. This trend must be in the reverse direction.

From another perspective, the current taxing system believes in collecting money from the haves and giving them to have-nots. This is not the right philosophy as the haves harvest the results of their efforts while the have-nots are punished because of their inactivity and passivity. In contrast, those who challenge the production must be taxed. The owners of idle savings pose the primary challenges to the production as they don't introduce their savings into the economy. Those who horde their money must be fined through taxing.

**The Fifth Reason:** The rule we came upon before: on equilibrium, the relative money marginal utility equals the relative marginal utility of its substitutes.

$$\frac{MU_m}{r} = \frac{MU_x}{p}$$

Now, if we arrange the relative marginal utility of every commodity in order of magnitude:

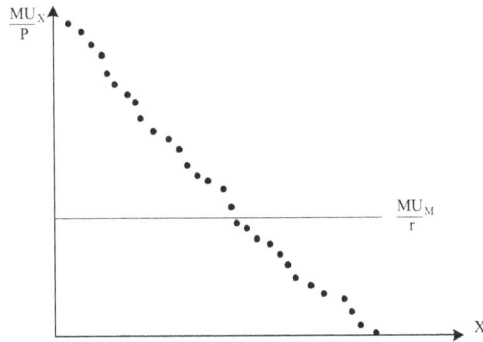

Figure 4.1: The relative marginal utility of money-substitute commodities

Every commodity whose relative marginal utility surpasses the relative marginal utility of the money $\dfrac{MU_m}{r}$ has been demanded and thus produced while those commodities whose their relative marginal utility falls below their mark have not gone on demand. As a result, demands for these commodities will take the form of money to be held by individuals. Consequently, unemployment exists in proportion to this idle money.

In other words, relative marginal utility of the money $\dfrac{MU_m}{r}$ becomes an impediment to the production of money substitute commodities and establishes a relative marginal utility standard failing to meet which prevents demands for a commodity and thus that commodity will not reach the production stage. Therefore, one can argue that the money that is not take the form of demands and instead kept by individuals is the root of unemployment. We thus can claim that the rich are responsible for the conditions of the poor since they don't spend their money. Moreover, the money saved by individual is the primary contributor to unemployment and thus those who horde money must be fined through taxing.

We have already cited five reasons for taxing the money. The fifth is the subject of our focus:

This rule has already been established:

**"On equilibrium, the relative marginal utility of money equals the relative marginal utility of its substitutes"**

$$\frac{MU_m}{r} = \frac{MU_x}{p}$$

Any changes in any constituent of this relation disrupt its balance, as a result of which the economy starts to modify. Changes in these variables proceed to re-establish this relation and restore a new balance point to the new relation.

For example, if individuals' tastes vary during the balanced state for some reason and the demands go up for certain commodities, this relation will go out of balance. As a result, the enhanced marginal utility of commodities increases $Mu_x$:

$$\frac{MU_m}{r} < \frac{MU_x}{p}$$

Here, the relative marginal utility of money-substitute commodities has surpassed that of the money and thus the individuals have been encouraged to exchange their money for money-substitute commodities. In other words, a sum of money is replaced with some substitute commodities. Since the utility of both the money and its substitutes diminish, increased demands for money-substitute commodities decrease their marginal utility (Mux) on one hand and increase their prices ($\rho$) on the other hand. In addition, decreased demands for money enhances its marginal utility ($Mu_m$) while the interest rate (r) starts to go down. These four changes prompt decreases in the right side of $\dfrac{MU_x}{p}$ while the left side of $\dfrac{MU_m}{r}$ increases to re-establish the relation above.

In another example, let's assume that this relation is balanced:

$$\frac{MU_m}{r} = \frac{MU_x}{p}$$

Now, if we add to the sum of money, the money marginal utility decreases according to $MU_m = B\dfrac{1}{M/_{Ny}}$ Thus, the previous relation will go out of balance:

$$\frac{MU_m}{r} < \frac{MU_x}{p}$$

Thus the relative marginal utility of money-substitute commodities surpasses that of the money. As a result, a number of money-substitute commodities for which no demand were in place before now are demanded and the individual tend to replace money with its substitutes. For this, the marginal utility of money-substitute commodities starts to go down. Now the individual is more open to spend more money for every commodity which gradually leads to increases in prices. In addition, since the money marginal utility has decreased, there are lower demands for money and as a result less interest is paid to obtain money. Consequently, the variables of this relation start to modify ( $MU_x \downarrow, P \uparrow, r \downarrow$ ). These modifications steer the above-mentioned inequality towards restoration of the balance.

One thus can claim that economic variables constantly move in directions that help keep this relation balanced. In the event of any loss of balance, the economic forces attempt to restore the balance.

Since non-demanded, not-produced commodities as well as unemployment exist in proportion to the volume of idle money, the relative marginal utility of money-substitute commodities must surpass that of the money if stimulation of the production is intended. As a result of lowered marginal utility of money, demands for those commodities with smaller relative marginal utility tend to go higher and reach the production stage. For demands to be placed for money-substitute commodities, the phrase on the left side of this relation must get as small as possible:

$$\frac{MU_m}{r} = \frac{MU_x}{p}$$

We suggested that money must be taxed if decreasing the saving aspect of the money and increased production are intended. Let's study the effects of taxing the money on this fundamental relation. Taxing the money does not bring about changes in the right side of the relation while the left side changes. If the money is taxed, the positive utility of keeping the money and the negative utility of the tax exist at the same time in the numerator of the fraction. Here two costs are imposed at the money in the denominator of the fraction; one the interest rate as the costs of the missed opportunity and the second the tax levied on the idle money. If money is taxed in the original balance condition, the balanced relation will be as follows:

$$\frac{MU_m - MU_t}{r + t} < \frac{MU_x}{p}$$

In other words, individuals demand commodities whose relative marginal utility is lower than that of the money. As a matter of fact, the imposition of tax on the money shortens the left-side phrase and thus individuals tend to supply their idle money to demand those money-substitute commodities whose relative marginal utility was lower than that of the money. As a result, these commodities start to be produced.

Therefore, some money-substitute commodities which previously had no demands get into the production cycle. The quantity of such production depends on the perceived power of the tax and how it can shorten the left-side phrase. The higher this perceived power and the shorter the left-side phrase, the more the commodities whose relative marginal utility is higher than that of the money (after being taxed) which prompts higher demands and increased production.

Due to increases in demands for and the production of certain commodities, on one hand the price of substitute commodities goes up and on the other hand their marginal utility goes down. Also, since a part of the money goes idle, the marginal utility of the money increases while the interest rate is reduced. These variations push this unequal relation in the direction of balance restoration in a new point:

$$\frac{MU_m - MU_t}{r+t} = \frac{MU_x}{p}$$

We have moved from the initial balance to new balance via tax imposition. Money is less idle in the new balance state compared to the initial one and thus more commodities are demanded and produced which ultimately decreases the unemployment and steers us to the optimal economical point.

Let's elaborate on the point through an example. On balance, the relation below was in place before taxing the money:

$$\frac{MU_m}{r} = \frac{MU_x}{p}$$

If we assume that $\frac{MU_m}{r} = 40$, then all the commodities with a $\frac{MU_x}{p}$ less than 60, 50 or even 40 will be on demand to be produced while the demands for those commodities with $\dfrac{MU_x}{p}$ of less than 40

$(\dfrac{MU_x}{p} < 40)$ will not exist.

Now let's assume that the tax imposed on the money in such a way that $\dfrac{MU_m - MU_t}{r+t} = 20$. Here, the special relative marginal utility of money will go down to 20 from the initial 40.

$$\frac{MU_m - MU_t}{r+t} = 20 < 40 = \frac{MU_x}{p}$$

Therefore, in addition to previous commodities, other commodities with a relative marginal validity ranging from 40 to 20 will be demanded and produced until their relative marginal validity reaches 20.[1]

$$\frac{MU_m - MU_t}{r+t} = 20 = \frac{MU_x}{p}$$

Now, only those commodities with a relative marginal utility of less than 20 will not be demanded. Therefore, more commodities were demanded and produced via tax imposition to help reach the new balance. As a matter of fact, through tax imposition, those commodities with a relative marginal validity ranging from 20 to 40(

---

[1] For the sake of simplicity, suppose that marginal money utility and interest rate do not change.

$20 < \dfrac{MU_x}{p} < 40$) will be added to the inventory of the commodities already produced. Unemployment will decrease in proportion to the new produced commodities which push us to the optimal point.

But where is the optimal point? I hope I have managed to convince you about the detrimental impacts of the idle money on the economy and that imposing tax on this type of money is the best way to get them back into the economic cycle. Now, the question is how much tax should be imposed on the economy? In other words, how the tax-on-money rate must be determined to restore the whole idle money to the economic cycle?

We have already shown that commodities are demanded and produced up to:

$$\frac{MU_m}{r} = \frac{MU_x}{p}$$

In other words, to a point where relative marginal utility of money-substitute commodities equals that of the money. We then showed that imposing tax on the money prompts more demands for production of money-substitute commodities up to the restoration of the balance below:

$$\frac{MU_m - MU_t}{r+t} = \frac{MU_x}{p}$$

Although idle money has decreased while the production has increased in contrast, there is always a limit on demands for money-substitute commodities and their production. Now if we wish to produce the commodities with the smallest relative marginal utility, the left-side phrase must be as small as possible and goes zero in the optimal state. Then we have:

$$\frac{MU_m - MU_t}{r + t} = 0 < \frac{MU_x}{p}$$

It means that the last commodity with the smallest relative marginal utility will keep being produced until the utility of money-substitute commodities is zero. According to the above-mentioned relation, the left-side phrase is zero in the optimal point. In other words, the optimal point is where the relative marginal utility of the money is zero. It is an effective point at which the whole money enters the economic cycle in form of demands, there is no shortage of demands and the employment is in full status.

But, on what conditions the left-side phrase will be zero? When the tax is imposed in such a way that the resultant marginal utility (the suffering) $(MU_t)$ equals the money marginal utility $(MU_m)$ and counteracts it:

$$\frac{MU_m - MU_t}{r + t} = 0 \rightarrow MU_m = MU_t$$

Here, the tax-induced suffering equals the joy of keeping the money. In general, the utility of keeping the money is zero which makes the individual indifferent to keeping or spending the money:

This leads us to this rule:

**"If the maximum demands for and the production of money-substitute commodities are intended, the tax must be imposed on the money in such a way that its utility (suffering) equals the marginal utility of the money"**

Here, the individuals exchange the money with every commodity (even with the smallest positive marginal utility). As mentioned earlier, this delivers a force to money in order to enhance its velocity. As a result of imposing tax on the money, the velocity of the money will reach its maximum which eliminates its saving incentive aspect.

We can arrive at the same conclusion via taking another road: as indicated before, money must be channel for transfer of values. We hit a problem when money found utility by itself. Thus the tax must be imposed in such a way that the resultant marginal utility (the suffering) equals the net money utility and counteracts it in order to re-assign money to its original task:

Another question is posed now: What tax-On-money rate has these characteristics? In other words, what rate of tax-on-money can produce a marginal utility (the suffering) equal the net money utility?

First let's describe the mechanism of borrowing money. Any individual that borrows money and repays it on an interest rate does so in the belief that the interest they obtain at least equals the extra charge paid as the interest rate. Now let's see how the income and the costs of the borrower are calculated:

The borrower can benefit from this money in two ways: either they spend it on an economic undertaking and thus make gains equal the economic result (R). In addition, the inflation detracts from the purchase power ($\dot{P}$) of the money to be repaid and thus a lesser value money must be paid. Thus the borrower will as well benefit in proportion to the inflation. The income of the borrower may obtain from the borrowed sum will be:

R+P= the rate of the income obtained from each unit of the borrowed sum of money

Let's see what costs the borrower has to pay for. The borrower must repay their debts according to the current interest rate and thus the costs of the borrower are:

r= the rate of the cost contracted for each unit of the borrowed sum of money

To make individuals willing to borrow money, the basic income must cover the associated costs. In other words:

$$r = R + \dot{P}$$

Which is associated with Fischer's relation:

However, the imposition of tax on money means that the borrower has to pay the tax apart from the interest rate as they are now the owner of the money. Therefore, the cost rate of the borrower is:

r+t= the cost rate of the borrower for each unit of the borrowed sum of money

To make individuals willing to borrow money, the basic income must cover the associated costs. In other words:

$$r + t = R + \dot{P}$$

Now we can figure out the optimal tax-on-money rate: this rate must be equal to the sums of rate of return and inflation rate. Therefore, the optimal tax-on-money rate must be equal to the rate of rate of return and inflation ($R + \dot{P}$) as the interest rate is zero now and will be eliminated from the economic system.

$$\begin{cases} r + t = R + \dot{P} \\ t = R + \dot{P} \end{cases} \rightarrow r = 0$$

In other words, if we impose a tax equal to the sums of rate of return and inflation rate, then the interest rate will be eliminated from the economic system.

Let's elaborate on the issue from the perspective of the lender (money owner). The lender believed that the borrower had to pay them an interest rate equal to that of the income (the sums of rate of return and inflation rate) because the interest was the reward regardless of the money ownership. Now the tax is in play, keeping the money has its own expenses and thus the individual is ready to lend their money interest-free if this income equals the income arising from ownership of the money.

Let's give an example to illustrate the point. Suppose that the sum of the rate of return on the economy and the rate of inflation is 10%. If the tax rate on money is set 9%, the lender will skip 10% of his income, so as not to pay 9% of the taxing cost. Therefore, if he lends money he will suffer a 1% loss. As a result, the lender will only be willing to lend money if he can cover the loss by an interest rate of 1%. However, if the interest rate is less than it, he will refuse to lend money. In other words, the person requests a percentage interest to lend his money under these conditions.

On the other hand, the borrowed expect an income rate equivalent to the sum of the rate of return on the economy and the inflation rate (10%), and if the tax rate is 9% as long as the interest is 1%, he is willing to borrow money and if the interest is higher he will refuse to borrow money.

Given the lender's and the borrower's decisions, if the sum rate of return on the economy and inflation rate (10%) and the rate of tax on money is 9%, the interest rate will be determined as one percent so that both the lender and the borrower be willing to make the deal.

$$r = (R + \dot{P}) - t$$

Now, if the rate of tax on money is 10% instead of 9%, the lender, on the one hand, will skip a 10% income (the sum of the rate of return on the economy and the rate of inflation) and, on the other hand, he will not pay a 10% cost (tax rate) and this it makes no difference for him to keep or land his money with zero interest and he will be willing to lend his money with zero interest. On the other hand, if the tax rate on money is 10% rather than 9%, the borrower is willing to pay 10% cost (the tax rate on the money) because the money yields a 10% income for him (the sum of the rate of return on the economy and the inflation rate). In this case, the other person is no longer willing to pay interest, and he will be willing to borrow this money only with a zero interest rate.

Therefore, on the one hand, in equilibrium, the rate of return on money (the sum of the rate of return on the economy and the rate of inflation) should be equal to the rate of cost of money (the sum of the tax rate on money and interest rates). If the tax rate on money equals the sum of the rate of return on the economy and the inflation rate, both lenders and borrowers are willing to make a deal at zero interest rates.

In fact, if there is this tax rate on money, the money owner will be quite happy to borrow his money and receive the same amount next year, because if this money remains with him, he should pay tax with a rate equal to his income from the money. So lending money and receiving it next year without interest is absolutely more cost effective. In contrast to today's state of affairs, in which money borrowers are in a state of urgency and weakness, and who demand borrowing money earnestly, in the new state of affairs (by imposing a tax on money), the owners of the money are in a state of emergency and are seriously seeking a person who will take their money and return it the next year without paying any interest and will be completely satisfied with this exchange.

In the new format, everyone avoids saving the money and instead attempts to push the money away to those who are able obtain the highest efficiency from it. As a result, talented and innovative are most likely to receive these sums who then contribute to the flourish of the economy. It is now possible for new ideas to develop and the creativity of innovative individuals bring around newer and more advanced commodities. More factories are founded and the market will be filled with new industrial products. More lands are farmed and there will be an abundance of crops and agricultural products. Houses, villages and towns will be established and improved one after the other. This type of tax eliminates the interest rate which in turn decreases the operation costs. In addition, even lower-rate of return businesses is cost-effective which prompts increases employment and production. In general, a surge will take place in the economy never recorded before.

Therefore, if the tax imposed on the money equals the sums of economic rate of return and the inflation rate, the interest rate would be eliminated. On the other hand, we know that the economic rate of return rate equals the sums of population growth and productivity growth or ($R = \dot{N} + \dot{A}$) and thus the optimal tax-on-money rate is:

$$t = (\dot{N} + \dot{A}) + \dot{P}$$

We had this relation before:

**"The rate of money publication must be equal to the sums of population growth and productivity growth to keep the money marginal utility and prices constant and make the inflation zero"**

In other words:

$$\dot{M} = \dot{N} + \dot{A} \rightarrow \dot{P} = 0$$

On one hand the optimal tax-on-money rate is equal the sums of the population growth, the productivity growth rate and inflation rate and on the other hand if the rate of publishing money is equal to the sums of population growth and productivity growth, the inflation will be zero. Thus we have:

$$\begin{cases} t = R + \dot{P} = \dot{N} + \dot{A} + \dot{P} \\ \dot{M} = \dot{N} + \dot{A} \rightarrow \dot{P} = 0 \end{cases} \rightarrow t = \dot{N} + \dot{A}$$

We thus come to this rule:

**"The optimal tax-on-money rate is equal the sums of the population growth and the productivity growth which makes a zero interest rate"**

This argument could be summarized as follows: The rate of money publication must be equal to the sums of the population growth and the productivity growth to make the inflation zero while the optimal tax-on-money rate must be equal to the sums of the population growth and the productivity growth to make a zero interest rate and eliminate the inflation and the interest rate:

$$\begin{cases} \dot{M} = \dot{N} + \dot{A} \\ t = \dot{N} + \dot{A} \end{cases} \rightarrow \begin{cases} \dot{P} = 0 \\ r = 0 \end{cases}$$

The optimal policy is that the growth rate of the money volume must equal the sums of the population growth and the productivity growth while the tax-on-money rate must be equal to the sums of the population growth and the productivity growth to eliminate the inflation and the interest rate:

We already have seen this relation:

$$r = R + \dot{P}$$

Thus the economic rate of return tends to zero when the economy is in its optimal state or when the inflation and the interest rate have been eliminated:

$$\begin{cases} r = R + \dot{P} \\ r = 0, \dot{P} = 0 \end{cases} \rightarrow R = 0$$

As long as the economic rate of return is positive, the economy will continue producing up to the last positive- rate of return commodity. The rate of return will be zero at the optimal state. We indicated earlier that the economic rate of return was in proportion to the sums of the population growth and the productivity growth. The economy will move on so long as these two factors which are dubbed the engines of the economy remain positive.

Previously, the interest rate was a limit to production rate of return. In other words, the production was cost-effective as long as its rate of return would surpass that of the interest rate. However, now there is no interest rate, the production goes on as long as the rate of return is positive.

The question we have to ask: will the economy reach the optimal point via imposing tax on the money? Imposing tax on the money neutralizes the added value of its savings and sets the idle money in motion. This money has two options: either goes to productive investments or unproductive investments. As noted in economic growth models, the sums of idle and unproductive money is zero in the optimal point and the whole saving is dedicated to the productive sector. Thus the tax-on-money policy must be complemented by some tax policies on the unproductive sector.

Making policies for the unproductive sector is necessary if we wish to prevent migration of idle money to this sector. But how much this tax must be? This tax must be set in a way to suppress any net efficiency of investment in such sector. Therefore, this tax must equal the rate of return of this sector to make it zero.

Generally speaking, after imposing taxes on both the money and the unproductive sector, the last commodity with the smallest marginal utility will be demanded and the last commodity with positive production rate of return will be produced. To resolve unemployment and achieving the optimal point, imposition of tax on both the money and the unproductive sector is suggested to enhance the $\phi$ value.

Although the science is yet to find a way to travel to the future, we believe that if tax-on-money policy (along its complementary policies) had been adopted, the human would made such huge advances in all fields, matching the advances the current monetary system can bring us during the next one thousand years. If tax had been imposed on money over the past one hundred years, we would have been able to see the advanced commodities and the facilities of the next millennium at this time, here and now. In other words, the human had made such great advances at the turn of the third millennium in building houses and factories, manufacturing of industrial and agricultural machinery, scientific innovation and advances and generally creation of the wealth that it will just happen at the turn of the next millennium with the current monetary system. In other words, had tax been imposed on the money, we would have had capitals equal to a thousand years in the future.

Taxing the money not only affects the production, but also profoundly impacts the distribution process. In fact, if tax had been imposed on money over the past one hundred years, the income distribution would have been so fair now that every justice-based establishment was thinking about now and promised it to its followers. In other words, if tax had been imposed on money over the past one hundred years, there would not have been such large income gaps and uncompromising differences between individuals in terms of using the wealth and thus the facilities and means would be divided bases on the creativity, talent, efforts and innovation of individuals.

In general, the following economic policies are proposed for achieving the optimal state:

The rate of increases in the money volume must equal the sums of the population growth and the productivity growth to keep the money marginal utility constant and eliminate the inflation. In addition, tax must be imposed on the money equal to the sums of the population growth and the productivity growth to remove the interest rate from the economy. The tax-on-money policy must be complemented by tax policies on the unproductive sector to help the economy achieve the optimal point.[1]

---

[1] The writer expresses his readiness to orally explain all the theories and the contents of the book in your university. He also will be ready to explain the practical method of collecting monetary tax and the mechanisms of monetary tax system in person. (m.ansarinasab@vru.ac.ir)

www.ingramcontent.com/pod-product-compliance
Lightning Source LLC
Chambersburg PA
CBHW080720220326
41520CB00056B/7209